Instant
INTERVIEW

Instant
INTERVIEWING

BRIAN CLEGG

**KOGAN
PAGE**

To Gillian Fagg of British Airways for introducing me
to interviewing by excellent example

First published in 2001

Kogan Page Limited
120 Pentonville Road
London N1 9JN
UK

Stylus Publishing Inc.
22883 Quicksilver Drive
Sterling VA 20166-2012
USA

British Library Cataloguing in Publication Data

A CIP record for this book is available from the British Library.

ISBN 0 7494 3388 4

Typeset by Jo Brereton, Primary Focus, Haslington, Cheshire
Printed and bound in Great Britain by Clays Ltd, St Ives plc

Contents

1 Conversation with a focus   1

Why this book?	3
Why instant?	3
How the book works	4
Should we interview at all?	4
The structured interview	4
Information	5
Environment	5
Selling	6
Nerves	6
Aggression	6
Note taking	7
Recruitment precursors	8
How many interviewers?	9
Recruitment – alongside the interview	9

2 Foundation skills   11

Using the foundation skills	13
2.1 Understanding the job	14
2.2 Setting criteria	15
2.3 Sifting applications	16
2.4 The perfect CV	18
2.5 Planning key questions	19
2.6 Meeting and greeting	20
2.7 What do they look like?	21
2.8 Note taking as you talk	22
2.9 Graphical notes	23
2.10 Open questions	24
2.11 Journalists' tricks	25
2.12 Your body	26
2.13 Non-verbal replies	27
2.14 Assessing test results	28
2.15 Simple option evaluation	29
2.16 Sophisticated option evaluation	30

2.17 Comparing apples and oranges   31
2.18 Using silence   32
2.19 Turning up the pressure   33
2.20 The top 10 list   35
2.21 Pareto   36
2.22 Breathing is good for you   37
2.23 Breaks   38
2.24 Taking up references   39
2.25 The offer letter   41
2.26 Recovering rejection   42
2.27 Scheduling interviews   43
2.28 Fair comparisons   44
2.29 Feedback   45

3 Information checklist 47
    Why information?   49
    The checklist   50

4 Environment checklist 57
    Why environment?   59
    The checklist   60

5 Selling checklist 67
    Why selling?   69
    The checklist   70

6 Question file 77
    About questions   79
    Selecting from the menu   79
    Managing the flow   80
    General personality questions   81
    Skills questions   83
    Business awareness questions   85
    Teamwork questions   87
    Leadership questions   89
    Manageability questions   92
    Self-starter questions   95
    Creativity questions   98
    Shock questions   100
    Analytical thinking questions   102

7 Other sources 105

      Finding out more   107

      General interviewing   107

      Being interviewed   108

      Information and knowledge   108

      Selling   109

      Motivation   109

      Stress management   110

      Time management   111

      Non-verbal communication   112

Index   113

CONVERSATION WITH A FOCUS

WHY THIS BOOK?

Interviewing skills are essential for any manager or professional, whether engaged in an interview-intensive occupation like recruitment, or in traditional line management. Yet all too many interviewers have had little or no training. An interview could be for recruitment or performance appraisal. It could be exploring the causes of a business problem or getting the truth from a potential supplier. The aim of this book is to provide the skills you need to interview effectively, whether you are starting from scratch or brushing up on a much-practised art. Generally, recruitment interviews are used as examples, but the skills have a much wider application.

An interview is a conversation with a focus. It is designed to extract information from the interviewee. This isn't as simple as it sounds. In most business conversations the other parties will have their own agendas, and even if there is no attempt at concealment, few of us are good enough communicators to put across everything we need to say pithily and comprehensibly. It isn't enough to listen to what the interviewees want to tell you; the interviewer has to probe, to direct and to go beyond the words to get as close as possible to the truth.

WHY INSTANT?

Interviewing is a stylized form of conversation, and as such requires preparation. But realistically you are rarely given enough time to do so. The need to interview might be dropped on you the night before. Many of us are expected to interview on top of our ordinary work. It's a crucial exercise, but one that inevitably gets pushed down the priority stack. Most interviewers outside a Human Resources department undertake the task occasionally and in the cracks between the other aspects of their job. It's not ideal, but it's the way things are. What's more, interviewing is a skill that many companies assume you will learn by osmosis. I was lucky that the company I first interviewed for provided me with a training course, but that isn't the norm.

When such an important activity is treated in this way, having an instant boost to your interviewing skills is highly beneficial – especially if you get little warning of being dropped into the interviewing hot seat. This book is designed to give you the core skills of the interviewer and to provide a toolkit of requirements and questions to launch you into an interview with confidence. *Instant Interviewing* is a chance to give interviewing the importance it should have in the time you've actually got available. The simple structure makes it easy to get just what you need in the limited time you've got.

HOW THE BOOK WORKS

After this introduction, there is a chapter of foundation skills – the basic requirements to be a good interviewer. This takes the form of a series of quick exercises that can be fitted in as and when you have the time. The next three chapters are annotated checklists to help with preparation for the interview, followed by a collection of subject-oriented lists of questions as a guideline for some approaches to take.

The final chapter gives information on further reading for interviewers – not just around the core topic of interviewing, but in some associated fields that will make for better interview performance.

SHOULD WE INTERVIEW AT ALL?

There is now a good body of research indicating that interviews alone are not highly effective as a recruitment selection method. Admittedly, some of those making this observation are responsible for the development and marketing of psychometric and other tests, but there certainly seems to be some evidence that many interviews are flawed. They remain, however, extremely popular, and most employers put a lot of faith in them.

I would argue that this apparent paradox can be overcome by improving the quality of interviewing. I suspect that those who denigrate the interview have not had much experience of management. Interviews are certainly not perfect, but they give an essential insight into the nature of the interviewee that no number of tests and questionnaires can entirely resolve. However, most interviews could be improved greatly, which is in part the reason for existence of a book like this. It's also true that most interviews can be helped by supportive evidence from tests and group exercises, and that a small interviewing panel of (perhaps) three people will be much more effective than an individual interviewer. But we shouldn't be too hasty to knock the interview. Like all human processes it is flawed, but done well it delivers.

THE STRUCTURED INTERVIEW

One form of interviewing that is growing in popularity in recruitment is the structured interview. This uses a set list of questions, delivered in exactly the same way with each candidate. The structure enables better comparison of applicants and, the theory goes, results in more accurate outcomes. It is indubitably a more scientific approach to interviewing. Nothing in this book either requires structured interviews or makes them unsuitable, but I have some doubts about their widespread use. I have nothing against having a structured section in an interview, but in most circumstances, an organic interview that follows the interviewee's responses will produce more depth. This requires a different style of preparation and note taking if it is still to be thorough, but is still preferable if the interviewers are suitably trained and competent.

INFORMATION

The first of the checklist chapters is on information. Information is the currency of the interview. Your role as interviewer is to extract information from the interviewee. Note the crucial distinction between information and data here. Data is a set of neutral facts. Take a recruitment interview. The interviewee's date of birth, his or her examination results, a list of employments – these are all data. Information tells you more; it is data plus interpretation, or data plus context. Information doesn't just tell you what your interviewee's exam results are, but why they are what they are, and what they signify for your requirement.

Some of the information and data you require will be taken directly from the interviewee in face-to-face conversation. It is certainly here that much of the interpretation and context will be applied to turn data into valuable information. But it would be very inefficient to extract every single fact from the interviewee on the spot. Some preparation, absorbing and putting the information you can obtain before the interview into context, will be very valuable in getting the most out of your limited interview time.

ENVIRONMENT

The second of the checklist chapters covers the interview environment. All too often, little thought is given to how the interview takes place and where it is located. It may be that your office, or the little interview room down the corridor, is the ideal place, but don't assume it. And when you have your interview set up, do you assume that all will be well with the environment, or do you take an active hand to make sure that it works for you and for your interviewee? The environment does matter if you are to make the most effective use of your interview time.

SELLING

It can seem strange that the third checklist chapter is about selling, but interviewing is a complex process (as is the case with practically any human interaction). Even if it were true that your only relationship with the interviewee was to pull information from them, you might like to sell them on the benefits of the interview to make sure that they give you as much as they can. However, most interviews fit into a context beyond the information itself. A recruitment interview is not only about selecting a candidate for a job; it is about selling the company to the candidate. An internal performance appraisal is giving a message to the staff member (anything from 'We desperately want to keep you' to 'I think you'd be more comfortable working somewhere else'). An interview with a supplier is part of building a working relationship; similarly a fact-finding interview will often be with people you need to work with in the future. The selling chapter is a reminder that interviewing is a two-way process.

NERVES

From the interviewee's point of view (particularly if this is a recruitment interview), you, the interviewer, are in a position of power. The interviewee will often be nervous, but will assume that you are calm and collected without a care in the world. This isn't a bad thing – it doesn't help to be interviewed by someone who doesn't seem confident and assured. For many of us, though, it is going to be far from the truth. An interview, especially the first interviews you perform, can be as nerve-racking for the interviewer as they are for the interviewee.

There is a pair of stress management techniques in the next chapter to help you to deal with these nerves, but the main weapon you have is your attitude. Think of all the positive benefits of doing the interview. It's a chance to talk to people – something most of us enjoy. It's a harmless situation from your viewpoint; you are in control. While keeping the professionalism and skills needed to make it an effective interview, try to think of it more as a structured chat.

AGGRESSION

Some companies and individuals use aggression as part of their interview technique. In theory this is to see how the interviewee stands up under pressure. But in reality it's hard not to see many aggressive interviews as thinly disguised sadism, where the interviewer abuses his or her position of power.

This doesn't mean that you shouldn't be firm in an interview. We've all heard interviews with politicians where the interviewer hasn't stuck to the point, and it is painfully frustrating to have the politician evade the question without ever answering it. Nor does it mean you can't stretch the interviewee. An interview I used to perform for the Operational Research department at British Airways required the interviewee to answer an apparently simple technical question that tested his or her ability to think through what their knowledge really meant, rather than simply recite back what they had been taught. I have known interviewees run out of the interview room in tears as a result of that question. But they had not been bullied or mistreated.

There's a need to remember that the way you treat an interviewee impinges on the selling aspect of recruitment. If I were a great candidate for a job and the interviewers bullied me, I would take great pleasure in telling the company's representatives what to do with their job when it was offered. Would you really want to work for a company that treats you like that? What does it say about how the company is likely to treat you in the future? There are perfectly straightforward mechanisms like role-plays to test how individuals react under pressure without abusing them in an interview.

NOTE TAKING

An essential in interviewing is being able to concentrate on the conversation: what the candidate is saying and how he or she is saying it. Yet, at the same time, you want to be able to return to the detail of what was said after the interview. It is not practical to rely on memory for this, particularly if you are involved in a series of interviews; the possibility of being clear exactly what was said in each one is almost negligible. Unfortunately, the need to concentrate on the interviewee and the need to take notes are in conflict.

In theory, perhaps the ideal is only to take steering notes yourself. These are the notes you will need to make sure that all the relevant questions are asked during the interview. Operating in this way, you would either tape the interview and run through it later, or have someone else take detailed notes for you. Unfortunately, both these techniques are labour intensive, and interviews are often conducted with limited timescales and resources. What's more, someone else's notes will never represent exactly the same picture that you would have gained yourself. If you are to take the detailed notes yourself, find ways that you can do this with the minimum interference with your conversation. We will look in the next chapter at making graphical keyword notes – it will also help if you can practise note taking without looking at the paper too often.

RECRUITMENT PRECURSORS

While the focus of this book is the interview itself, it is worth considering some of the surrounding paraphernalia that will influence the interview, particularly in the recruitment process. In many recruitment environments there are far more potential recruits than there are vacancies. Ideally everyone would be interviewed. The fact is, flawed as it may be, the interview is still an essential component of the ideal selection process. But it is neither practical, nor cost effective, to interview 1,000 candidates for a single job. Some form of sifting is required.

The starting point in using sifting has to be an understanding that it is going to fail you. Whatever technique you use to sift will remove some of the best candidates for the job. The hope is that there will be enough suitable candidates left – but don't fool yourself into thinking that you are being wonderfully scientific. Sifting is a pragmatic tool, and a very blunt one.

Some sifting techniques used by large companies verge on the ridiculous. A good example is handwriting analysis, which has no properly verified scientific basis. Rather than spend money on handwriting analysis, you would be better picking every tenth application, or everyone whose surname begins with C – it is just as likely to give a good result, and is both much cheaper and much quicker.

An apparently more logical sifting mechanism is academic results. You might, for example, insist that all applicants have a degree. This is not bad as sifting goes – many degrees indicate some ability to reason, and all show that the candidate has had the perseverance to attend the university or college for the required terms. However, there are some aspects of academic results that need closer examination. For example, a first class degree may indicate a candidate with limited social skills – a check on his or her wider experience would be worthwhile. Similarly, while a second degree or masters in a practical subject is promising, a doctorate needs to be treated with suspicion. A doctorate often shows a strong interest in knowledge for its own sake, which is rarely a good sign in a practical job. Narrow focus is all very well in academia, but can be dangerous in the real world.

If you have to sift before an interview, see if you can use a more human judgement. At least take the time to read the application and look for the signs of a good CV and form. These will be discussed further in the next chapter. This doesn't have to take long, and will beat any mechanical filtering.

What, though, of telephone interviewing? Is this a sensible compromise, perhaps for a second level of sifting? Again, approach with care. Telephone interviews can be valuable, but can also be extremely misleading. Unless you are interviewing for a position where good telephone skills are high on the requirements list, you are liable to unfairly bias the interviewing process to those who are very comfortable on the phone, a fairly small cross-section of the population. Make sure the interviewee has time to prepare – book a telephone interview, don't call out of the blue. As with aggression, remember the potential for projecting a negative image. Cold interview calls suggest that your company is disorganized or sneaky – neither exactly excellent sales pitches.

HOW MANY INTERVIEWERS?

Generally, the interviewee is a lone figure, unless this is the kind of interview that requires a professional advisor like a lawyer to be present. However, the interviewer has a wider choice. The interview can be a cozy one-to-one chat or an ordeal before a long line of panel members. The choice is yours.

To an extent this choice is limited by practicality. In many companies it simply isn't practical to have loads of interviewers, even if it was desirable. But there may still be a degree of choice. For an internal interview, perhaps assessing annual performance, there is rarely a need to have more than a single interviewer. But for a recruitment interview, a larger interviewing panel is probably ideal. I would recommend from practical experience that having three people works best. A human resources or personnel person, an interviewer that either would be the recruit's boss, or is of a similar level, and a more senior interviewer, ideally with wide experience of interviewing.

In such a triumvirate, the human resources individual can provide technical guidance and observe human characteristics. The junior interviewer, who should be asking most of the questions, provides the contextual questions. And the senior interviewer has an overview and will add some more general business questions. When it comes to deciding on the outcome, such a group can come to a more measured decision, not overly influenced by a single person's biases.

If there are more interviewers than interviewees, care needs to be taken to make sure that the experience is not intimidating. A loose grouping of chairs, for instance, is less threatening than having the interviewing board ranged in a straight line behind a vast, imposing table.

RECRUITMENT – ALONGSIDE THE INTERVIEW

In recruitment, interviewing will often not be the only tool that is used. A corporate interview can involve a whole battery of tests, role-plays and group exercises. The aim is to get the best all-round picture of the individuals who have applied. Some of these tests are very valuable. Personality profiles, such as the Myers Briggs Type Indicator, give a good guide to how an individual will interact with others in a team, as does the observation of a group or a role-play (however artificial the situation). Reasoning tests can help to indicate suitability for certain occupations. (These don't always have to be formal tests. When recruiting code breakers for the secret Bletchley Park centre, 'Station X', during the Second World War, the British government used expertise with crosswords as one of its indicators.) But it is probably unwise to put too much effort into this backup activity, because that's all it is. All the evidence is that it is the interview that will make or break the selection. If someone has a great interview, the interviewer will tend to ignore the test results. If it's bad, they're out, however good the tests and role-plays.

2

FOUNDATION SKILLS

USING THE FOUNDATION SKILLS

Each of the short exercises in this chapter will help to give you some of the basics needed to interview successfully. You can work through each or cherry-pick those that represent your personal weaknesses – but check that you are happy with all of them.

Interviewing is a broad-based skill. You will need to dip into communications skills, time management, stress management and other disciplines along the way. Because of this, a number of the exercises below come from these associated disciplines, but each is worthy of a book in its own right. See Chapter 7 for a range of references on supporting skills as well as on interviewing itself.

2.1 | *Understanding the job*

Preparation None.
Running time 10 minutes.
Resources Job description.
Frequency Once.

It may seem a self-evident truth that you, as interviewer, need to know the details of the job you are interviewing for, but it is surprising how difficult in can be on the spot to translate a job description into the requirements for a successful candidate. Get hold of one of your company's job descriptions for a job you don't know too much about. If this isn't possible ask a friend to write one for you. Take a couple of minutes to read it through, then try to jot down a description of a successful applicant. Don't do this in job description language – make it as if you were writing a personal letter, describing an acquaintance. What would they be like? What sort of questions would you need to ask to establish whether a particular applicant was like this? If an interviewee asked you to summarize what the job entailed and how it benefited the company in a few sentences, what would you say?

Feedback Getting practice at absorbing a job description before an interview is very valuable. Each time you interview for a job you haven't interviewed for before, you should undertake this exercise. A job description may be extremely valuable, but it does not usually translate directly into the foundations of an interview. By spending a few minutes really getting into the nature of the job beforehand, you can leave your concentration free to listen to what the interviewee has to say. In some circumstances there will be no job description. Still undertake this process, but base it on your understanding of the job. When this is the case, it is important that you test your understanding with the job's stakeholders, specifically the new boss (if it's not you), peers and customers (in the broadest sense).

Outcome By having a clear picture of the implications of the job on the person required, you can build effective foundations for your interview.

Variations This exercise is labelled as a one-off, but could benefit from several tries, especially if you are interviewing for several different types of job. It should also be used in practice as described.

2.2 | *Setting criteria*

Preparation *Understanding the job* (2.1).
Running time 5 minutes.
Resources Job description, notes.
Frequency Once.

This exercise flows on from *Understanding the job* (2.1). Once you have a picture of what the job is about, you need to establish the criteria by which you are going to pick out a successful candidate. These are the measures that describe how well an individual comes up to your requirement. Look through your output from the previous exercise and the original job description. Come up with at least three and no more than seven measures against which each candidate can be rated and that represent the most important factors for being successful in the job.

Feedback Having these measures will allow you to do an objective comparison of the candidates. Note that they cannot make the decision for you. They can only provide guidance. Sometimes, other factors will push you in a different direction. Sometimes, for instance, the objective criteria are overruled by gut feel – in such circumstances there are one or more hidden criteria that are influencing the decision. One of the valuable outputs of this exercise is that if you disagree with the objective assessment you can try to establish just what those hidden measures are.

Note also that each of the criteria may not be equally important. When we come to the *Sophisticated option evaluation* exercise (2.16), this will be taken into account.

Outcome With a clear set of criteria it will be much easier to compare candidates. See the two option evaluation exercises, 2.15 and 2.16.

Variations This exercise is labelled as a one-off, but could benefit from several tries, especially if you are interviewing for several different types of job. It should also be used in practice, developing criteria that apply to each job you interview for.

2.3 | *Sifting applications*

Preparation None.
Running time 10 minutes.
Resources Application forms (if available).
Frequency Once.

It is often the case that you will have more letters, CVs and application forms than you can deal with. Getting practice at sifting these quickly to cut them down to a manageable quantity is an important pre-interviewing skill. For the purposes of this exercise you need either a set of applications, or some equivalent pile of documents, that you can work through quickly. If you haven't anything else, get hold of a heavyweight newspaper, and use the articles as if they were applications. You can't use these as effectively, but can approximate to the process.

Before undertaking the exercise, you will need to be clear just what it is that you are looking for in an application, and particularly what are the exclusion criteria. Do you have any minimum academic or experience criteria? To get some further criteria, look through the first couple of applications in detail. Are there aspects of the application that you can quickly pick up that you might use to include someone in or out? Look at the presentation. While you aren't looking for professional styling (at least for most jobs) you ought to have an easy visual exclusion criteria if an application looks terrible. Look out for similar, easy-to-spot exclusion criteria that fit your particular requirements. (If you have to do the exercise with a newspaper, you will have to use quite different criteria. Exclude anything about sport, or with obvious grammatical errors. Keep in anything with a scientific topic, or whatever. Use your imagination.) Now run through all the rest of the applications as quickly as you can. Don't spend more than 20 seconds on each. Finally, revisit your exclusion pile, giving each a little longer. Be prepared to reinstate a few that have redeeming features that you didn't spot on the first pass.

Feedback This approach can seem highly arbitrary, but the fact is you need to sort out a workable subset of the applications, and you need to be able to do this quickly. Sad though it is for the individuals who are rejected, it doesn't honestly matter if you do exclude some good applicants as long as you are left with other equally good candidates to choose from. The visual exclusion criterion is particularly easy to apply quickly, so worth having. If you feel any concern that these individuals are being excluded on an arbitrary measure, bear in mind the message a candidate who produces an application that is messy or illegible seems to be giving. 'I don't care much about the job, and can't be bothered to put much effort into this.' Does this sound a desirable interviewee? Arbitrary though this is, I suspect it will usually be more effective than the widely used criterion of a certain level of academic achievement.

You may also have other small details that trigger suspicion. I have always worried about the personalities of applicants who either write only in upper case, or have clearly written each line of text along a ruler – but perhaps I am being arbitrary. Certainly I would not recommend going into pseudo-science like handwriting analysis. If you need to be that arbitrary, you might as well select the first X number of applications to arrive, or everyone whose surname begins with C.

Outcome Practice in swiftly cutting down the number of applicants to a practical number for interview is essential when popular jobs may have hundreds or even thousands of applicants. Develop the skill.

Variations None.

2.4 | **The perfect CV**

Preparation None.
Running time 20 minutes.
Resources Your CV.
Frequency Once.

Take your existing CV (résumé), or whatever equivalent information you have about yourself, and transform it as much as possible into the ideal CV. Here are a few tips, but make sure the result matches your own requirements:

* Avoid being too technical; the CV may be filtered out by the HR department if they don't understand it.
* Keep it short – one page if possible, two at most.
* Include a brief summary, a reverse chronological experience guide (with more weight on recent and impressive roles), details of education and any special skills and characteristics.
* Don't go mad with layout. Use one font (or at most two, the second for headings). Keep the layout simple and straightforward.
* Unless requested, don't include a photograph of yourself.
* Accompany the CV with a covering letter emphasizing the key reasons why you are ideal for the post.

Feedback There is no other CV that you know more about than your own. By using this as a model for your appreciation of what makes a great CV, you can make it easier to assess and consider other CVs. This isn't just a matter of the sort of sifting described in 2.3, but includes extracting the essential information and getting a good picture of the individual from the CV.

As a side issue, you may improve your own CV to your own benefit, but this isn't the point of the exercise, which is to gain a better feel for a great CV.

Outcome An understanding of the CV as a communication vehicle is an essential pre-interview skill.

Variations If you have employees, see what you've got on file for them as CVs. What picture does it give you? How does it compare with what you know about them from experience? How could it be improved?

2.5 | *Planning key questions*

Preparation *Setting criteria* (2.2).
Running time 10 minutes.
Resources Job description.
Frequency Once.

Looking at a particular job and the criteria developed in exercise 2.2, devise a series of key questions that might be asked to cover the essential information you require. Make sure there's between 10 and 15 questions. Of these, note one that would make a good opening question. If there isn't an obvious contender, add a specific, general purpose opening question.

Feedback There is nothing worse than an interview conducted from a rigid list of questions. It lacks any sense of flow. If a candidate says something that needs following up, or makes a comment that naturally leads on to a different question, it is very clumsy to ignore this and stick regardless to the list of questions that you devised before the event.

So what is the point of this exercise? Because the next most terrible possibility in an interview is that the interviewer dries up. He or she suddenly realizes that it's impossible to come up with another question. There is an embarrassing silence. The interviewee very quickly gets the impression that your company is unprofessional, while you will probably get a totally distorted view of the interviewee.

By having a series of key questions planned, you can be comfortable that your opening question is prepared, and have a series of other questions available. You don't have to use these questions at all, but they are ready and waiting should the need arise.

The key questions should not be seen as appearing in any particular order. If a candidate's answer makes it natural to ask the sixth question immediately after the first, that's fine. Let the flow of questions fit organically with the conversation. It's probably best, therefore, to have the questions in some form of visual structure like a mind map (see *Graphical notes*, 2.9) so that it is possible to jump around more easily. Again, if you reach the end of the interview and you haven't used all your key questions that's fine, as long as the ground has been covered. Use a quick scan of your key questions to ensure there isn't a last question you need to ask.

Outcome Getting into the habit of putting together a list of key questions before an interview in an easily accessible form can be very helpful in making the interview flow smoothly and effectively.

Variations None.

2.6 | *Meeting and greeting*

Preparation None.
Running time 5 minutes.
Resources None.
Frequency Once.

The first few minutes of an interview, beginning at the point where you first meet the candidate, can be highly influential, both on the candidate's opinion of the company and yours of the candidate. Assemble a checklist for these first few minutes. It might include some of the following:

- Handshake and smile – seem welcoming.
- Say who you are and what your role is.
- Give the candidate an outline of what is going to happen. Remember that you are in a position of power – you know what is going to happen. To the candidate, everything about the surroundings and the process may be strange. Give some reassurance through information.
- If the candidate has had a long journey, offer him or her the opportunity to freshen up first.
- Get the candidate seated comfortably. Don't play silly games, for example, putting the candidate on an uncomfortable chair or one that is much lower than your own.
- Ask if the candidate would like a glass of water, or cup of coffee or tea.

Feedback You will probably have local needs that vary these suggestions, but the point is that the candidate should come across naturally in the interview, rather than being in a constant state of fear about the surroundings and what is going to happen next. The aim of an interview is to have a directed and assessed conversation with a human being, not to undertake an interrogation. It is probably best if you highlight bodily needs (freshening up; a drink) rather than leaving it to the candidate to ask, or you may end up with someone who becomes increasingly uncomfortable because he or she was too polite to mention it.

Being nice to the candidate in this way isn't being weak. Not only will you get a more natural response, but bear in mind that high quality candidates are liable to be offered a number of jobs. You are in competition for them, just as much as they are in competition for your job. It doesn't do any harm in improving your chances of getting an offer accepted if you make the experience a pleasant one for the candidate.

Outcome Good meeting and greeting will ensure that candidates think the best of you and are well prepared to do their best in the interview proper.

Variations None.

2.7 | *What do they look like?*

Preparation None.
Running time 10 minutes.
Resources Newspaper.
Frequency Once.

Go through a newspaper and find half a dozen pictures of individuals with very different modes of dress, hair style and so forth. Look at each in turn, imagining that this person has turned up for a middle management interview that you are conducting. What do you feel about the individual? Would you start off favourably or unfavourably inclined towards them? How much do you think his or her appearance would influence an otherwise average interview?

Feedback There is no doubt that physical appearance has a big influence on us. What is important is that you analyse your own reactions, understand them and keep them in balance in a real interview. Beware of any bias as a result of physical attractiveness or unattractiveness to you of the individual. This isn't always a matter of tending to favour a physically attractive candidate; sometimes an interviewer will underrate an attractive candidate in an attempt to seem unbiased. Your reaction to choice of clothing, hair styles and colouring, body-piercing and tattoos should reflect not your own personal inclinations, but the requirements of the job.

To insist that a telephones sales operative dresses in business attire is as bizarre as the way that early radio announcers were required to wear dinner jackets to make a broadcast. However, staff exposed visually to customers (external or internal) will need to have an appropriate dress sense. And it is reasonable to make some assumptions about how seriously the candidate is taking the interview from the way they have attempted (or not attempted) to match your company's public persona. Famously, at a first meeting of representatives of a joint venture between Apple Computer and IBM, the laid-back anarchistic Apple staff wore suits and the tight-laced East Coast IBMers wore jeans and T-shirts. Both made the right decision – they were matching the perceived dress style of their new partners. The meeting (if not the joint venture) was a great success.

Outcome How a candidate looks at the interview is important, but the measures should be down to the job requirements and your company's desired image, not any personal preferences.

Variations None.

2.8 | *Note taking as you talk*

Preparation None.
Running time 10 minutes.
Resources Pen and paper.
Frequency Several times.

Note taking is an essential in interviewing, but you don't want to take your concentration off the candidate or what is being said. There are two skills that need to be practised here – making notes as you interact with the candidate without losing the thread of your conversation, and making notes without looking at the paper.

The next time you are involved in a business conversation or meeting, try taking notes in this way. Try to let the notes flow without taking your attention off what is being said.

Feedback You may well find to start with that your notes are virtually unreadable, hence the need for practice. Equally, you will find that the words come faster than your ability to keep up. Keep at it, though – this is a skill that improves with practice. Once you are reasonably happy with this stage, you can move on to graphical notes (see 2.9), which will need a little more of your concentration to construct (so you need to be even better at taking notes while keeping up a conversation), but which are much easier to revisit during the interview.

Outcome Without good note taking there is no way you will even be able to assess a single candidate for a job an hour or two later, let alone a whole range of candidates. This has to be got right.

Variations It isn't practical to make graphical notes (see 2.9) without looking at the paper, but even if you are using that (highly recommended) technique, you may well have to scribble a note without looking, then fit it into your structure when you have a moment's pause.

2.9 | *Graphical notes*

Preparation None.
Running time 20 minutes.
Resources Pen and paper.
Frequency Once.

Good note taking is an essential for interviewing. You need to be able to take notes while keeping most of your attention focused on the discussion. Even more importantly, you need to be able to find a note without losing concentration. Graphical notes are ideal for this requirement. In this exercise, take about 20 minutes to make graphical notes of the main points you know about interviewing.

Start at the centre of a page and draw a circle containing the core of the issue. From this, radiate out branches that represent the major themes of the issue. From each of these draw progressively lower and lower level themes.

On each of the branches write one or two keywords above the line to say what that issue is. For instance, one branch might be experience, splitting into jobs, education and social, with education splitting into school, college and postgraduate.

In general, try to make the image organic. Start with larger and fatter branches at the centre, moving to smaller and smaller ones and eventually to twigs at the extremities. If you are already familiar with graphical techniques like mind mapping, don't go overboard. This isn't the right environment to be using different colours and fancy graphics; speed of capture is more important than memory retention.

Feedback Note taking while keeping focus improves with practice. This exercise is one-off in terms of learning the basics of visual note taking, but should be repeated by putting the technique into use. Every time you go to a meeting, for instance, try taking notes this way (whether or not you need any) as practice.

Outcome Better note taking will result in staying on top of the interview, giving you the ability to really listen to what is being said, but also to be able to jump back to your key questions at a moment's notice. It's a must.

Variations There are various alternative note-taking strategies but none can compare with this approach for interviews. See details of my *Instant Brainpower* and the *Mind Map Book* by Tony Buzan, the inventor of mind mapping, in the Information and Knowledge section of Chapter 7 (page 108) for more on effective note taking.

2.10 | *Open questions*

Preparation None.
Running time Five minutes.
Resources None.
Frequency Once.

Closed questions can turn an interview into a nightmare. These are the sort of questions that prompt a one word answer, giving hardly any information. Any closed question can be asked in an open form, inviting a fuller answer. So, for example, instead of asking, 'Did you enjoy your last job?' (answer: 'yes' or 'no') you could ask, 'How do you feel about your last job?' In theory you could get the answer 'good', but you are much more likely to get revealing detail. Rephrase these closed questions as open ones:

- Did you enjoy your last job?
- Is our company better than its competitors?
- Were you fired from your last job?
- Are you happy with our terms and conditions?
- How many jobs have you had?

Feedback That last one isn't a 'yes' or 'no' question, but it's still closed. Even professional interviewers can fall into the trap of asking closed questions. Keep an eye out for them in TV or radio interviews. If you do get a 'yes' or 'no' answer to a question, give yourself and the interviewee a moment's silence (see *Using silence*, 2.18). Many interviewees will naturally begin to expand on their answer. The more experienced interviewees will be aware of the danger of closed questions themselves, and do the opening up for you. During that pause, rephrase the question as an open one. If the interviewee doesn't open it themselves, either re-ask in the open form or just say, 'Could you tell me a little more about that?' or, 'Could you expand on that?'

Note a second advantage of the open question that may well have emerged from your rephrasing. For example, the question, 'Were you fired from your last job?' is a loaded one. If instead you asked something like, 'What prompted you to leave your last job?', you get more information, but also don't irritate the candidate by implying that they might have been fired if they weren't.

Outcome Keeping your questions open will ensure that you get the maximum flow of information from the interviewee.

Variations When you are in interviews, try to spot any closed questions you tend to ask. Pick up on them and consciously look for alternative phrasings to make them open. Occasionally, you may use closed questions intentionally to test a candidate's verbal skills. There are a few examples of this in Chapter 6.

2.11 | *Journalists' tricks*

Preparation None.
Running time 5 minutes.
Resources Someone to talk to.
Frequency Regularly.

Interviewing is not solely a business activity; it's the meat and drink of journalists, whether working for the print or broadcast media. Make use of the standard journalists' checklist in your questions:

- What?
- Where?
- Why?
- Who?
- When?
- How?

Don't just ask what they did; ask them who they did it for, when it was done, where they did it, how they did it, and most penetrating of all, why they did it.

Two more journalistic quickies. Have an opening question and a couple of difficult questions prepared. Ask the same question several times if you feel an answer is being evaded and you need to find out why the evasion is taking place. If necessary, ask directly: why don't you want to answer?

Feedback The five 'Ws' and an 'H' list of questions is a mental prompt, not a script. The idea is not to ask all six questions about every point that comes up – it would quickly get tedious and repetitious. Instead, they are there so you can be aware of possible gaps in your knowledge, and choose the appropriate and important ones to fill in a fuller picture.

Outcome By using journalistic techniques you can maximize the chances of getting to the pertinent information.

Variation Watch some interviews on the TV and see how the interviewer explores points. Look for reasonably lengthy, searching interviews – a heavyweight political programme would be a good source.

2.12 | *Your body*

Preparation None.
Running time 10 minutes.
Resources Mirror, clipboard, large book, pen.
Frequency Once.

The interview is a two-way process of communication, not a one-way flow from the interviewee to you. All the time, as you speak to the interviewee, you are putting across non-verbal messages. It is important that you do so in a controlled way, rather than accidentally.

Get hold of a mirror and prop it up so that you can see your face and your upper body in it from a comfortable seating position. Get hold of a clipboard, a large book and a pen. Spend a few minutes talking to yourself (as interviewee) in the mirror – bearing this in mind, you need to find a location where you won't be observed. During this pseudo-conversation, try to notice as much as possible what you look like in the mirror. At different points in the conversation, make some notes on the clipboard, look up something in the large book, yawn and grimace.

Feedback We all have habitual actions when in conversation, some of which may be giving entirely the wrong message to an interviewee. Be aware of your posture. Being slumped can make you seem bored or not interested. Facial expressions that might be designed to suppress a yawn or deal with an itchy nose can seem dismissive. And too much time looking away from the candidate – whether at your notes or other documents, or even at the ceiling or out of a window – can again signal a lack of interest. It may be your tenth interview of the day, but it's the candidate's first and only chance. Don't let the way you look and the messages your body gives put them off. Instead, make sure you give good encouraging signs – frequent (but not staring) eye contact, smiles, nods, leaning forward a little in your seat. Also make sure that you look relaxed. Don't cross your arms across your body – open up to the candidate.

Outcome Giving the right non-verbal communication is very important, as anyone can be put off by negative signals.

Variations Conduct the exercise with a stooge instead of a mirror. Get feedback on how he or she felt.

2.13 | *Non-verbal replies*

Preparation None.
Running time 20 minutes.
Resources TV.
Frequency Once.

Your body (2.12) concentrated on the non-verbal messages you were giving out. Be very aware also of the non-verbal communication from your interviewee. If you stick to words alone, you are ignoring a large part of the information being communicated to you (this is one of the reasons that telephone interviews don't make particularly effective job interviews).

Over the next week, when watching TV, look out for interviews. Watch the interviewee's body language. What message is coming across from his or her posture, facial expression and non-verbal sounds? Make quick notes on four or five different interviewees.

Feedback Some basics to look out for. How does the person sit? Are they slumped (low energy) or upright? Are they leaning forward (showing interest) or leaning back (detached). How do they use their hands (watch out for cultural variances here)? Is their facial expression at odds with what is being said? Is there good eye contact, keeping in touch with the other person much of the time, but dropping away regularly so that it does not become a stare? Does the interviewee seem evasive or wary? How can you tell? Are there sympathetic responses? Is the interviewee reflecting the interviewer's posture? Is the interviewee smiling and nodding acceptance? Does the interviewee use regular non-verbal sounds to put across agreement and understanding?

One thing to be aware of here – non-verbal communication is an important part of your conversation with the interviewee, but don't regard it as some sort of visual lie detector. Most candidates for professional roles will be familiar with the basics of body language, and will make a conscious effort to look convincing. It isn't always easy to force a particular non-verbal message, but it is often possible. Even so, this is a major part of the communication process, and it is certainly harder to fake the whole spectrum of non-verbal communication than it is to lie verbally.

Outcome To miss out on the wide bandwidth of non-verbal communication would be a great shame.

Variations If you don't know much about body language and want to go beyond the comments above, see page 112 in Chapter 7 for further reading on the subject.

2.14 | *Assessing test results*

Preparation None.
Running time 10 minutes.
Resources None.
Frequency Once.

If you are interviewing for a large firm, the chances are that you will have to merge the output of your interviewing with the results of one or more test results. A typical professional battery of tests might include verbal reasoning, personality profile, numerical skills and any technical aptitude required.

Put together a list of five significantly different jobs that you are familiar with. Against each, list any tests that you think would be useful. For each job/test combination, note down how you would use the outcome of the test in coming to a decision about this individual. Perform this exercise before reading on.

Feedback The most important consideration when dealing with test results is not to be blinded by science. Don't let the fact that these results have concrete numbers against them give them an unnecessary gloss and importance. Test results should support the interview, but never supplant it.

Good applications of a test result are directing and fine tuning. If you know from your interview that you are going to offer an individual a position, but have several posts that might be appropriate, tests like a personality profile can help to assess how the individual would fit within a particular team or working environment. If, on the other hand, you have one post and several candidates, who were all excellent in interview, you may need test results to push you in one direction or another.

To some extent you might use test results to filter – for instance, requiring a certain level in a reasoning test – but in general the interview should have more weight. Anyone can make a mistake in a test, but few can appear totally different in a good interview to their actual performance.

Outcome Tests are very valuable, but shouldn't be overrated. Understanding how to make best use of the results is important if tests are part of your interviewing armoury.

Variations Try performing the tests yourself (and look at your results) before making decisions on others based on those tests.

2.15 | *Simple option evaluation*

Preparation *Setting criteria* (2.2).
Running time 15 minutes.
Resources Notepad, pen.
Frequency Once.

This exercise, developed from one in *Instant Negotiation*, is useful wherever you have a number of options to choose between. In this instance, you are selecting candidates for a job.

List the candidates on a piece of paper. If there are more than three or four, try to eliminate some immediately as totally unacceptable. For the purposes of the exercise, use a hypothetical job and a number of real people that you know.

Now list the criteria by which you will decide between candidates (see *Setting Criteria*, 2.2). What will you use to distinguish them? Again, keep to a handful of the most important criteria.

Finally, score each candidate against each criterion. Either use a 1–10 scale or a High/Medium/Low (H, M, L) scale. Combine the results: with a 1–10 scale this means simply adding the scores together. For High/Medium/Low, add how many H, M and L scores each has.

This should give you a ranking of the candidates according to these logical criteria. With High/Medium/Low scoring, this ranking could be on high scores first, then medium, then low, or by giving each a weighting. However, the ranking shouldn't be used as a fixed decision, but rather a guide to put alongside your intuition. If your gut feel differs from the logical assessment, try to see why. Are there criteria you are ignoring? Are some criteria much more important than others?

Feedback Using a simple mechanical comparison like this will give you a first cut at how the candidates stack up, but more importantly, it will also help you to understand how you are coming to a decision if you disagree with the assessment.

In practice, it is usually the case that not all criteria are equally important to the job, so before using this technique in anger, move on to the next exercise, *Sophisticated option evaluation.*

Outcome The systematic approach will both help to make the decision more rational and to understand how you are making your decision.

Variations See *Sophisticated option evaluation* (2.16).

2.16 | *Sophisticated option evaluation*

Preparation None.
Running time 20 minutes.
Resources Notepad, pen.
Frequency Once.

Like the previous exercise, this is developed from one in *Instant Negotiation*, and the technique can be used when deciding between any type of option – in this case candidates for a job. Sometimes, criteria aren't enough to decide between candidates. You need to be able to give different weightings to say that, for example, experience is twice as important as qualifications. The process used is much the same as in *Simple option evaluation* (2.15), but will take a little longer.

List the candidates on a piece of paper. Even more so than with a simple evaluation it is important you restrict the list to perhaps three or four. Then list the criteria by which you will decide between candidates. What will you use to distinguish them? Again, keep to a handful of the most important criteria. Before going any further, weight the criteria. Give the first criterion the value 1 and give each other criterion a value that reflects its relative importance compared with that key criterion – for example, if it's half as important, give it a value 0.5. If it is twice as important, make it 2.

Finally, score each candidate against each criterion using a 1–10 scale and multiply each score by the criterion weightings before adding up the results.

This should give you a ranking of the candidates according to these logical criteria.

Feedback Using this more sophisticated approach you should, in theory, be able to read off just who is going to get the job. However, the ranking should only be a guide to put alongside intuition. If your gut feel differs from the logical assessment, try to see why. Are there criteria you are ignoring? Are your weightings incorrect? There could be a number of reasons for diverging from the 'logical' criteria. It might be experience overruling theory, or simply that you are taking in a complex mix of signals that you can't quantify as criteria. Either way, this process provides a simple guide, a starting point for discussion and an understanding of how and if you are diverging from your stated criteria.

Outcome A systematic approach ensures that you have considered all the options, and that you are picking one with a conscious awareness of the criteria by which you will make the choice – the outcome is a more rational, thought through decision.

Variations If the numbers are getting a bit of a strain, you may find it helpful to use a spreadsheet instead of paper. See the free software section of the Creativity Unleashed Web site (**www.cul.co.uk/software**) for a sample spreadsheet to handle a recruitment option evaluation in this form.

2.17 | *Comparing apples and oranges*

Preparation None.
Running time 2 minutes.
Resources None.
Frequency Once.

It's convenient to think of a series of interviews for the same job as a production line, matching up a series of near-identical products against the packaging and choosing the best. In practice, it's rarely that simple. Specifically, you are liable to have the unenviable task of comparing metaphorical apples and oranges.

Imagine you had two equally excellent candidates for a job. One has lots of experience and is very laid back, quietly confident about his abilities. The other has significantly less experience, but is better qualified and has incredible drive; she will clearly give 150 per cent to the job and will enjoy every minute. Spend a couple of minutes thinking about how you would make a decision between the two.

Feedback   It would be possible to perform an option evaluation (see 2.15 and 2.16) on the candidates. In fact, this would prove very useful to help to understand more about the different criteria that you are using. But you would still end up having to make a direct comparison of experience and qualifications, confidence and drive. In the end it will be necessary to have relative weightings for some very different properties of the individual. For instance, you might decide that experience is more important than academic qualifications, but that enough experience to prove competence combined with enthusiasm was better than lots of experience combined with a lack of drive. The essentials to dealing with apples and oranges are to be very sure of your criteria, how they combine and what your weightings are. Performing an option evaluation won't necessarily give you the answer of who to recruit, but it certainly can help with this understanding.

Outcome   Human beings don't come out of a mould; you will have to compare very different people with very different abilities, each of which may be more or less valuable to this particular job.

Variations   None.

2.18 | *Using silence*

Preparation None.
Running time 5 minutes.
Resources Someone to talk to.
Frequency Regularly.

One of the most effective tools of the interview is silence. Forcing yourself not to say anything can be quite difficult. You might have something you are just dying to bring up – but the point of the interview isn't for you to get going on your favourite topics. Or it may be that the interviewee seems to be struggling. You want to help him or her out, and so plunge in. Or maybe you can't cope with the silence. If so, you are a victim of this technique yourself, whether applied consciously or unconsciously.

Using silence is a technique that needs practice. Try it out in social conversations. Don't always plunge in with your opinion, or the story you desperately want to tell. Give the other person a chance to develop their argument.

Feedback A silence, except between people who know each other very well, is usually regarded as a social irritation. If nothing is being said, you start to feel that you are not contributing enough. You cast around, looking for something, anything to say. Often what comes out will be rubbish. Yet silence is a great technique for the interviewer. It may be that your interviewee is taking a moment to collect his or her thoughts. That's a good sign, not a bad one – don't ruin the moment by starting to waffle. Or it may be that the interviewee is feeling the pressure. It's cruel and unnecessary to actually attack them at this point, but to leave a silence is a neutral way to allow the pressure to build until the interviewee is ready to take action.

Silence has to be used constructively. After an interviewee has made a full and effective answer, there is little point in allowing them some silence. But if his or her answer is short, or is yet to appear at all, give silence a chance to work for you.

Outcome If you can overcome your natural tendency to fill in silence, you will have a great technique to encourage an interviewee to say more.

Variations To be effective, this technique needs to be in a one-to-one, or your co-interviewers need to know that your silences are used with intent. Similarly, when practising silence in conversation, you need a one-to-one environment to prevent someone else leaping in to plug that painful gap.

2.19 | *Turning up the pressure*

Preparation None.
Running time 5 minutes.
Resources None.
Frequency Once.

Many jobs involve an element of stress – sometimes decisions have to be made at great speed, with little time for careful consideration. Take a couple of minutes to consider what you could do in an interview to turn up the pressure without making the experience so unpleasant that the candidate won't want to have anything to do with your company. Jot down some thoughts before continuing.

Feedback Putting candidates under pressure has to be handled very carefully, bearing in mind that your job is as much to sell your company as it is to test potential employees out. It's fine for a candidate to come away thinking that your company was rigorous and made the process challenging. It is not good for candidates to come away thinking that you are a bully.

There are several opportunities to turn up the pressure. You can interview in unusual surroundings – anything from a hotel bar to a swimming pool. You can ask the candidate to take part in group exercises and role-play. You can use the sort of stress questions and analytical thinking questions that you will find in the appropriate sections of Chapter 6. And you can spring surprises on the candidate, bringing in sudden changes to the requirement. For example, you might ask them to work on a business problem, then halfway through change the circumstances.

This is all fine, but the important accompaniments are in attitude and in finishing. Some interviewers feel it puts more pressure on to be aggressive and even insulting in questioning. Do not do this. It doesn't matter how much you later assert that you were simply testing the individual; they will be left with a subconscious picture of you as an aggressor and a source of danger. This image (perhaps quite rightly) will also be applied to the company. The candidate simply won't trust the company in the future. Put an interviewee under stress, but don't accompany this with personal remarks. Whatever happens, make sure that you finish with a debriefing in which you explain why the particular approach was taken, and exude warmth about the individual and his or her performance. If you complete a gruelling task and finish with praise ringing in your ears, you will be positive about the whole experience. If you load all the human aspects up front, then put the candidate through a series of unpleasant experiences and send them straight off home, they will carry away an indelible negative image of your company.

Outcome   Working under pressure is a fact of life in many jobs. Feel free to test for ability to cope, but by doing so in a humane way, and making sure that the candidate goes away with a warm glow, you will not prejudice him or her against the company.

Variations None.

2.20 | *The top 10 list*

Preparation None
Running time 5 minutes.
Resources None.
Frequency Weekly.

This exercise is about time management. This is an essential if you are to take on interviewing on top of your normal job (as is usually the case), and if your interviews are to be supported by the information you need in the time available. The exercise is a variant of one of the many in *Instant Time Management* (see page 111 for more details). Note your top 10 concerns for the coming week. Many of these concerns will be driven by your focal activities, the most important things in your personal priorities. Put the list somewhere very visible. If you have staff, e-mail them a copy.

Whenever you start a task, glance at the top 10 list. Does the task influence your top 10? If it doesn't, you may still do it, but bear in mind its relative unimportance. If you are asked to do something that doesn't fit with your list and you are short of time, say 'no'. Next week, when you draw up your list, make sure there are changes. There may be ongoing priorities, but if everything stays the same from week to week you are stagnating.

Feedback If you are to interview properly it ought to be part of your top 10 list for the week. Making this the case should ensure that it is given appropriate importance and that, if necessary, some other activities are displaced. The visible top 10 list is a very powerful vehicle for time management, and that has much more impact than might seem possible.

Outcome The top 10 list cuts through your potential activities to the essentials. It's great both for work and at home. I was introduced to the idea of sharing your list with staff by Nick Spooner, MD of Internet commerce company Entranet. Nick used his top 10 list to communicate priorities to his staff and before long they all had their own lists in public view. This has significantly improved the company's effectiveness. A side effect of the top 10 list is to reduce irrelevant interruptions. A meaningful look at the list as someone comes close can cause them to reassess their priorities.

Variations None.

2.21 | *Pareto*

Preparation None.
Running time 5 minutes.
Resources None.
Frequency One-off.

Pareto is another exercise from *Instant Time Management* that is particularly valuable to the interviewer. When I first heard of this technique it was given the grand title Pareto Analysis – now it's more often called the 80:20 rule. The nineteenth century Italian economist Vilfredo Pareto discovered that 80 per cent of the wealth was owned by 20 per cent of the people. Since then, this 80:20 rule has been found to apply in many circumstances.

The importance to time management is recognizing that you can often achieve 80 per cent completion with 20 per cent of the effort. The final polishing takes a huge 80 per cent. Sometimes that remainder is vital. You don't want a nuclear power plant that's 80 per cent safe. However, for most tasks (could it be 80 per cent of them?), 80 per cent success is fine. The Pareto rule explains one of the reasons PCs can be such a waste of time. It's tempting to use all those exciting features of your word processor to continue to refine the appearance of your letter (or form, or spreadsheet, or whatever) with violently diminishing returns. When you are setting goals and milestones, wherever possible use an 80:20 target. Spend a few minutes checking through your schedule for the next few weeks. Are you applying 80:20?

Feedback For some of us, Pareto is absolutely natural. We are happy with approximate solutions that do the job. For others it is a real wrench, a 'botched job'. This technique is not an excuse for sloppiness, but a plea for accepting a very good result rather than striving for perfection. Would this preclude the great works of art, the great theories of science ever being developed? Maybe, but lots of great thinkers and artists work very quickly – greatness isn't always about nit-picking.

Apply Pareto both to your everyday tasks, to free up time to be able to interview (and to prepare for it), and to the interview itself to get the most out of the session in a practical time.

Outcome The potential for freeing up time is enormous. If you moved every-thing from perfectionism to Pareto you would free up 80 per cent of your time. This isn't going to happen, but there is still a huge potential.

Variations None.

2.22 | *Breathing is good for you*

Preparation Find a quiet place.
Running time 5 minutes.
Resources None.
Frequency Regularly.

Stress is a fact of life when interviewing. This exercise and the following one, taken from *Instant Stress Management*, can help you to project a better image – and to be more comfortable about the whole process of interviewing.

It's a self-evident truth that breathing is a good thing, but there's breathing and there's breathing. Firstly, as all singers know, there are two types of breathing – with the chest muscles and with the diaphragm. The latter is more controlled and gives you a much deeper breath, yet it tends to be under-used, particularly by those under stress. Try to feel that diaphragmatic breathing. Stand up, straight but not tense. Take a deep breath and hold it for a second. Your chest will rise. Now try to keep your chest in the 'up position' while breathing in and out. You should feel a tensing and relaxing around the stomach area. Rest a hand gently on your stomach to feel it in action.

Now lie on the floor or sit comfortably in a chair. Close your eyes. Begin to breathe regularly: count up to five (in your head!) as you breathe in through your nose. Hold it for a second, then breathe out through your mouth, again counting to five. Rest a hand on your stomach. Don't consciously force your rib cage to stay up now, but concentrate on movement of the diaphragm. Your stomach should gently rise as you breathe in and fall as you breathe out.

Feedback One of the great things about a breathing exercise like this is that it can be performed pretty well anywhere. It's easy to indulge in a five-minute breathing exercise in the run-up to an interview without being obtrusive.

Outcome The breathing exercise is simple and very effective at inducing calm, an excellent precursor to interviewing. What's more, it will help with your breath control if you sing or play a wind instrument.

Variations Do use this exercise before interviewing, but you may find it helpful to do it daily – some people recommend breathing exercises as much as three times a day.

2.23 | **Breaks**

Preparation None.
Running time 5 minutes.
Resources None.
Frequency Once.

This stress-relief tactic applies both to a day of interviews and to your whole working life. We've all been in the situation. You are working under pressure. Time is short and there is a huge amount to be done. And then you get a series of interviews to do on top of everything else. The temptation is to schedule all the interviews as tightly as possible, work through your lunch break and then work on into the evening to catch up, using regular doses of coffee to steam open your eyelids and keep yourself going.

Unfortunately, there is overwhelming evidence that this is not a great way to get the most out of your brain. The amount of information retained and the quality of your output drops off after time working at the same task. By taking a series of short breaks, much more can be achieved. There isn't a magic length for the chunks of time, but most people find that working between 45 minutes and an hour, with breaks of around five minutes, will overcome the deterioration.

In the few minutes allowed for this exercise, you aren't going to get anything practical done. Instead, take your next schedule of interviews and work (or invent one for the exercise) and rough out chunks and breaks. Then make sure you use your schedule.

Feedback It's very tempting to carry on if everything is going smoothly. But however well it seems things are going, your ability to remember and to reason will benefit from breaks. It's especially dangerous to do a series of interviews for the same job without stopping. The break should be something completely different, involving a different use of the mind. Having a discussion about the candidate with the other interviewers or reading the next candidate's application form doesn't count. Getting out in the fresh air for a few minutes and unwinding is ideal.

Outcome Breaking things into chunks makes a lot of sense, but it's human nature to forge on and try to get through, especially under pressure. It often takes tight scheduling to force yourself to take breaks to begin with, but persevere for improved output and less stress.

Variations Try different chunkings to see which works best for you. The natural tendency is to try for the longest chunks as these seem more efficient. It isn't necessarily the case that they will be best for you.

2.24 | *Taking up references*

Preparation None.
Running time 5 minutes.
Resources None.
Frequency Once.

Most employers ask for references to make sure that there is some match between what the potential employee has said and objective reality. You have a number of decisions to make here. Consider each of these questions and give an answer before moving on to the feedback.

- Should you take up references before or after making an offer?
- Who should you ask for references from?
- How can you make sure that you will get a speedy response?
- What should be covered?

Feedback A surprising number of companies take up references prior to an offer being accepted. This can be highly compromising for the individual: the current employer may not be happy that he or she is looking elsewhere. It is much more considerate to make an offer subject to references, and only take up the references once the offer has been accepted.

The ideal person to get references from is the individual's immediate superior. A reference from the HR department is only going to tell you about attendance and compliance with legal requirements; usually you want more. If the person wasn't previously employed, look for a trustworthy figure who would really know them – a tutor at university or a family friend in a high-trust job.

By the time you get to references, you will want the process to operate quickly and smoothly. If you are using a written request, make sure there is a return envelope with postage. But to get a quick response, it might be better to offer the opportunity to reply by fax or e-mail. Alternatively, you can see if it's practical to take up the references by phone. This way you can conduct a mini-interview and get a feeling for the depth behind the rather general statements that written references generally produce.

The aim of the references is to check the truth behind any claims of experience and qualification, and to establish the working characteristics of the individual. Sometimes, there will also be a need for security checks, such as police checks on an individual who will be working with children. Generally, though, references should not be about personal issues, but about how the individual would approach and perform the job, and how he or she would work with other people.

Bear in mind, by the way, that you have to take anything positive you are told in a reference with a pinch of salt. Sadly it is not unheard of for managers to give an individual a glowing reference with the intention of getting rid of that person. If you were told the truth you would not employ the applicant, and hence wouldn't take him or her off the manager's hands. Hopefully this doesn't often happen, but it certainly can.

Outcome References rarely tell you too much that's new and positive, but can flag up potential problems that aren't obvious from an interview. For example, the only way you are likely to find out that someone tends to promise and then not deliver is from his or her references. The exercise is worthwhile if handled correctly.

Variations None.

2.25 | *The offer letter*

Preparation None.
Running time 5 minutes.
Resources None.
Frequency Once.

Although it is good practice to make the initial offer verbally, as you can do this more quickly (both putting the applicant out of his or her misery and reducing the chances that your candidate will have been snapped up by another employer), the verbal offer should be followed up by an offer letter to ensure that there is a clear understanding of what is being offered (particularly important in the unlikely event of anything going wrong in the future). If you don't have standard letters generated by your HR department, spend a few minutes thinking through what an offer letter should contain. Note down your thoughts before continuing.

Feedback The letter should specify as much as possible to avoid any misunderstanding. Specific elements it should contain include:

- Company name.
- Job title and starting salary.
- Any conditions (such as satisfactory references).
- Outline of any bonuses, performance related pay and so on. Also criteria for how these will kick in over the first year.
- Outline of any other benefits, including pension and perks.
- Details of leave and how this will be phased in over the first year.
- Any relocation support that will be provided.
- Starting date, location and map.
- Who to contact if there are any queries.
- A copy with space for signature and date.

Outcome Fuzzy offer letters can result in disappointment and, at the extreme, legal action. Make sure that you are very clear about what you are offering.

Variations None.

2.26 | *Recovering rejection*

Preparation None.
Running time 5 minutes.
Resources None.
Frequency Once.

The recovery here is yours, not the interviewee's. Just occasionally there will be one superb candidate for a job and no one else worth considering. What should you do if this person rejects your offer? Give the matter a little thought and outline a strategy before continuing to the feedback section.

Feedback It may be that you feel that there are plenty more fish in the sea, and it's simply a matter of advertising the job again. This is fine. But it may also be that you have had several attempts and this is the only time you have had a great (or even, for that matter, acceptable) candidate.

Get in touch with the candidate. Ask if it would be possible to get together briefly before he or she definitively says 'no', as you feel that there could be some movement on the offer. He or she was obviously interested enough to come for the interview – surely it's only a matter of detail and you would like to explore that. If he or she says that another job has already been accepted, ask whether anything has been signed. Point out that offers are generally conditional – it is entirely fair for the candidate to have second thoughts at this stage. Surely, it's at least worth hearing what you have to say? Get together on ground of the candidate's choice – at your premises, at his or her home, or on neutral territory. Go in with a clear picture of how far you can afford to move on any of the variables you can change. Don't try to work this out on the spot. Start by pushing the ball into his or her court. Ask the candidate what would make him or her have a change of heart. This will give you a ballpark figure, although there may be a reluctance to say anything, to see what you have on offer.

When you do make an offer, use up around half what you have to play with in the first go. You need to prove that you are serious. After that, if necessary, give decreasingly smaller amounts away, making it clear that you are reaching a limit. Bear in mind that you have lots of variables, not just basic pay. You can offer much more reward based on performance, as well as cost-free options such as extra vacation and low-cost options, eg perks. Have a whole menu of changes available so that you can respond to the candidate's needs and wishes. Most of all, if you have to undertake this type of exercise, read one of the books recommended in Chapter 7 on negotiation.

Outcome You won't always get someone after a rejection, but the situation can often be turned around if you are serious enough about wanting the candidate.

Variations None.

2.27 | *Scheduling interviews*

Preparation None.
Running time 2 minutes.
Resources None.
Frequency Once.

One of the essential time management aspects of interviews is scheduling. All too often interviews are arranged in a tight series with perhaps five minutes between each. Say you had eight candidates to handle over a two-day period. Each interview will take between 45 minutes and an hour. How would you schedule the days? Take a minute or two to jot something down before proceeding.

Feedback My personal preference would be to arrange interviews at 9.30 am, 11 am, 1 pm and 3 pm each day. The 9.30 am start is to allow some time for preparation. You don't want to rush into the building and straight into an interview. It also gives the first candidate a chance to cope with unexpected traffic delays.

I have allowed 30 minutes between sessions. This allows you a chance to recover and have a drink, or to get out and have a short walk in the fresh air, but most importantly it allows for overrun. Almost always you will get some interviews that overrun, and these can have an unpleasant knock-on effect through the day. It gives entirely the wrong impression if you start an interview late. There is a longer gap at lunchtime. You ought to eat a (light) lunch, otherwise by mid-afternoon you will be flagging.

Ideally, I would have started the last interview around 2 pm. If you are interviewing all day, by the time you get to late afternoon you will not be giving the interview your best. As it was, allowing sufficient buffer time was more important, but if the interviews could be split over more days, I would consider making them all morning sessions. Interviewing a whole day at a time is exhausting, and is often impractical, with the need to keep getting back into the normal working environment. If you can confine interviewing to half a day, both the interviewing and your normal work benefits.

Four sessions in a day might not seem many – but these are long interviews. If it is necessary to squeeze more in, make sure that you keep a proportional amount of buffer time.

Outcome By not scheduling interviews too tightly you will get better performance from both interviewers and interviewees.

Variations None.

2.28 | *Fair comparisons*

Preparation None.
Running time 5 minutes.
Resources None.
Frequency Once.

If you are interviewing a number of people for the same post, perhaps across several days, you will need to put a considerable amount of effort into taking a balanced view across the different interviewees. Spend a few minutes thinking of the possible pitfalls to avoid in such circumstances. Jot them down before continuing.

Feedback Generally there will be some candidates who stand out more than others. This is fine if the reason that they stand out is their excellence, but all too often the cause is not so logical. Just the sequence of interviews can make a difference. Whoever came first, and (particularly) whoever you have interviewed most recently will stand out. It may be that a candidate simply has something that attracts your attention – he or she is very beautiful, or has a broken leg or a strange speech pattern. We can also be biased by underlying prejudices. It's no surprise to anyone when certain countries in Europe's Eurovision Song Contest vote for either their neighbours or countries with which they have ethnic connections. Similarly, we may be forced into an unbalanced view by the impact of some prejudice.

The latter problem can really only be dealt with by being extremely scrupulous and by using an interviewing panel rather than an individual. The timing-based problems can be helped by allowing time to consider each candidate immediately after his or her interview, rather than saving everything up to the end of the day. Such scheduling also provides greater buffer times in case something goes wrong.

Outcome It's not enough to assume that you will be fair; you need to make a conscious effort not to let any candidates stand out on any grounds other than competence.

Variations None.

2.29 | *Feedback*

Preparation None.
Running time 2 minutes.
Resources None.
Frequency Once.

It is not uncommon for a failed candidate to ask for feedback. Spend a minute or two thinking about whether this is acceptable and, if so, what should be done about it.

Feedback I have been involved in interviewing where it was company policy not to give feedback if an interviewee was unsuccessful, but this is not an ideal approach. You are making a major decision in a person's life, and they are quite justified in asking for reasoning. In some cases (for example, industrial tribunals and appeals), they may even have legal grounds for this request. Feedback is particularly important if the applicant was someone you would like to work for your company, but simply wasn't suited to the job (or there were too many good applicants).

Feedback should not be imposed, but it should be clear how to get it if required. The feedback ought to come from the line managers making the decision, not an HR professional, even if he or she was involved in the interview. This feedback should have a small number of clear and logical reasons. It should be phrased so that it does not seem to be a negative critique, but instead it should seem helpful advice for the future.

If given verbally, the feedback should start by giving the criteria for the decision, then you should encourage the applicant to explore his or her own shortcomings in these regards. This way there is much more likely to be acceptance of your decision. Only if the candidate stubbornly refuses to recognize any problems should you go on to explain what it was about them that made failure occur.

However poor the candidate's performance, don't send him or her out thinking that there is no future for them in employment anywhere, with anyone. Make it clear that he or she has good points, which would be of value elsewhere, but weren't a good match for this particular requirement. To make feedback possible, it is essential that you hold on to your interview notes for at least one year after the interview takes place. One final consideration – never give feedback on the spur of the moment. If a candidate gets in touch unexpectedly and asks for feedback, arrange for a time to do so in the future. You need preparation to make sure that the right message is given.

Outcome Feedback is an important courtesy that should be available to all applicants.

Variations None.

3

INFORMATION CHECKLIST

WHY INFORMATION?

An interview, as we have already established, is a conversation with a purpose. That purpose is to extract the appropriate information from the interviewee to match the interviewer's requirement. In job-related interviews, this is normally the information necessary to understand how the individual would perform in a particular job, though it will often involve the background information that answers, 'What kind of person is this?'

However, the candidate is not the only source of information, and to go into an interview unprepared is to risk the session being unstructured and uninformative. There's nothing worse than completing an interview and realizing that you are no more able to make a decision based on the information you have elicited than you were before the exercise. Getting access to appropriate information upfront and either absorbing it or having it readily available during the interview is an essential precursor, enabling you to ask the right questions and to get a full picture.

This chapter consists of an information checklist – a short list of information that you can check off before undertaking an interview – and some detail on each of the items listed. The checklist is divided into three sections:

- All – information that will be valuable in any interview.
- External recruitment – information that is particularly relevant when interviewing an outside job applicant.
- Internal interview – whether considering an internal job applicant or a career review.

It may seem that there is an awful lot of work needed before the interview, but being appropriately prepared is essential. Bear in mind that some of this material needs only to be covered once for any number of candidates. And by applying the Pareto technique (see 2.21), it should be possible to get together the essentials in each category without spending too long over it. It's certainly true that 15 minutes preparation for an interview will have a much greater effect on the value of the interview than adding an extra 15 minutes to the interview time.

THE CHECKLIST

ALL
- Goals
- Key questions
- Interview plan
- Interviewee's CV
- Application form
- Test results
- Job description
- Letter of invitation

EXTERNAL RECRUITMENT
- Details of interviewee's last company
- Information on your own company

INTERNAL INTERVIEW
- Interviewee's performance appraisals
- Conversations with boss, peers and customers

ALL

▌ *Goals*

This is the foundation of the whole interview, without which there is no direction; if goals are missing, the result is an unstructured meander rather than a practical, focused exercise. Goals are such an obvious requirement that it's surprising how often they are never formally stated. Getting the goals down in writing is very useful, as it ensures that the goals are thought through and that they are shared by the interviewers if there are more than one – don't assume that the goals are obvious.

In assembling the goals of an interview, you should be answering a series of questions. What is the point of the interview? What are you hoping to achieve? If the interview was a total success, what would be the outcome? Try to explore the requirement in more detail than simply 'to fill job X'. Why do you need to fill this job? What do you hope to get out of the interview process that would enable you to succeed?

From thinking through these questions, assemble a handful (no more than four or five) of key points that are your guiding force behind your activities. Keep each goal down to a single line, and make it comprehensible, concrete English, not vague concepts and sentiments.

▌ *Key questions*

For any particular job, for any particular interview whatever the context, there are liable to be a number of key questions. These are likely to include an effective starting question, then a series of questions highlighting the main points that you would like to cover. There is no need on the day to ask these questions in the form that you have written them out, or to ask them all, but the aim should be to provide a series of prompts so no essential requirement of the interview slips through the cracks. Having real questions written down rather than vague topics will help if, for some reason, you need another question under pressure and haven't time to construct one.

Ideally, such questions need to be laid out on paper in such a way that they can be easily accessed at a moment's notice while in an interview where you are liable to be giving most of your attention to the interviewee. It is helpful to have a specific section of your page with the questions listed, rather than scattering them among your notes. It can also help to use some form of graphical note taking (see exercise 2.9) to give the questions an element of structure.

▌ *Interview plan*

With your background information and key questions assembled, it is useful to put together an interview plan. This is a broad structure for the interview itself, choreographing the conversation from a starting point of introductions through to the closing words. It isn't and couldn't ever be a script – an interview is a two-way process, and should be shaped as much by the interviewee's input as it is by your intentions. However, this does not negate the value of having a plan. Not only does this ensure that you cover all the required areas, but it can be of value in returning to your thoughts after the interviewee has taken you off on a detour.

The plan is probably best structured in some organic form, like a mind map (see exercise 2.9), rather than as a set of linear notes, as this makes it easy to skip about in response to the interviewee's answers while still maintaining a good overall picture of what has been accomplished so far.

▌ Interviewee's CV

The CV (Curriculum Vitae) or résumé is essential pre-interview reading. Don't assume you can handle a CV on the spot during the interview itself. You will need to extract the information that is most relevant to your requirement, something that is very difficult to do as a background task while talking to someone else. Look for the questions that the CV generates. What does it say about the person's experience and its relevance to your requirement? What specific experiences does it mention that you need to ask more about? What characteristics has the applicant identified in himself or herself that are obviously considered important to the job? What characteristics might make him or her unsuitable for the job? What relevant qualifications does the person have? What do his or her activities outside work highlight in terms of personality, creativity and drive?

▌ Application form

Like the CV, the application form really needs to be mentally processed before the interview itself. Although it will often be the case that you are familiar with the style of the form and hence able to pick out key information more quickly than from a CV, it is still too much to expect in the course of an interview. If you want to use the form directly, highlight important information; otherwise, note down a summary of the key points. Again you should be looking for important background and questions arising. What did the candidate mean by this statement? How would this experience help or hinder performance?

▌ Test results

Many companies employ a battery of tests alongside the prime mechanism of the interview. Provided the tests are seen as ancillary rather than dominating, this is fine. The question remains, whether the test output should be part of your preparation for the interview, or considered separately afterwards, alongside the interview notes. (This assumes, of course, that the timing of tests is such that this is practical; sometimes logistics necessitate tests coming after the interview.)

Some HR professionals prefer interviewers to undertake the interview 'cold', unbiased by the test results, so that a more objective judgement can be made, which is then modified if necessary by the results. This is rather like the way that UK law requires an alleged criminal's previous record to be kept quiet until after the trial, so that it doesn't bias the jury's decision. However, if the interviewer is firm in the belief that the tests are merely corroborative, it can be useful to have the test results before the interview. Do they highlight particular weaknesses or strengths? Perhaps these should be investigated in more depth in the interview. Do the test results imply a preference for certain team roles? Exploring this with the individual in the light of the job that is up for grabs can be very enlightening. With a suitably professional interviewer, it is arguable that test results provide a useful component for the pre-interview information checklist.

▌ Job description

We have already looked at the need to be aware of the goals of the interview – an associated piece of information is the job description. This may be a formal document, or simply an assessment of the type of role the interviewee is likely to fulfil. In absorbing a job description before interview, look through the whole document, then pull out a number of details. What are the essential requirements for the job? What criteria could you use to choose between different candidates, given this job description? Are there any specific questions that the job description suggests? Make sure that you take a clean copy of the job description to the interview with you in case the candidate asks for one.

▌ Letter of invitation

This is an unusual component of this checklist, as the information is provided not to you, but to the interviewee. Unless your aim is to unsettle, it is very helpful to provide the interviewee with clear details of what will be happening in the interview process. This should start with good instructions on getting to the interview, and on timing. It should also give a little detail of who the interviewee is to see and what their responsibilities are, plus some information on any non-interview components, such as tests and group exercises. Enabling the candidates to be prepared for what is going to happen will make them more cooperative on the day and reduce nervousness.

EXTERNAL RECRUITMENT

▌ *Details of interviewee's last company*

Interviewees don't spring into being fully formed. Any background you can gain before the interview on their past can be helpful in assessing just what the interviewee is like, and can also influence some of the questions you are likely to ask in the interview. Find out something about the interviewee's last company (or university, or whatever). What size of company is it? What is it involved in? How does it do business? For an educational establishment, what sort of regime is involved? How will the candidate's work have been tested? What opportunities were there for real world experience? And so on.

Getting hold of this information can be easier than you may think. Most large companies will produce brochures about the company that can be obtained by contacting the company's publicity department or equivalent. You can see if you know anyone who used to work there, or perhaps your company already employs someone with the same background – what can they tell you? And the Internet can be a rich source of information. If you aren't familiar with using the Internet in this way, see *Mining the Internet* (details on page 108), a guide to the skills needed to make the most of the Internet as a personal and business information resource.

▌ *Information on your own company*

We have explored the reasons why it is useful to have information about the candidate's previous company. It is equally valuable to have absorbed information about your own company. To an extent this will contribute to your picture of the match of the individual to the job – the more you know about your company the better chance there is of making that match effective. However, having a good grasp of company information will also be valuable when it comes to your second role in an interview of selling the job and the company.

It should come perfectly naturally to you to describe exactly how the job fits in with the structure of the company, and to explain how the company benefits from the job. You should also be able to position the group or department in the company, and again explore its role. Make sure you can draw up a few simple diagrams to explain this. This will work much better than referring candidates to their position in a vast, unpalatable printed organization chart. It is also important that you appear competent by demonstrating an understanding of the company rather than looking up the answer to any questions in company guides and documents. By all means have the glossies for the interviewee to take away after the event, but try not to rely on them when talking about the job, the department or the company.

This is largely a requirement when dealing with external candidates, but in a large company you may still need localized departmental and group information.

INTERNAL INTERVIEW

▌ *Interviewee's performance appraisals*

In the specific case of an interviewee who is already employed by your company, you may have access to performance appraisals. Many companies, especially those operating reward and incentive schemes based on performance, will have regular reviews of how well the staff members are doing against a set of standard measures. While such measures can't be taken on face value – it's certainly not appropriate to choose a candidate by adding up the scores and selecting the candidate with the biggest number – the performance appraisal provides a short cut to be able to ask the candidate why a particular characteristic is considered a strength or a weakness. If you have access to a series of review results, you can also look for trends and ask why a particular characteristic appears to be in decline or in the ascendant. Make sure that it is acceptable within your company to use this information in this way; breaching confidentiality is no way to build trust.

▌ *Conversations with boss, peers and customers*

In an internal interview, you have an opportunity that simply isn't available elsewhere. You can talk to the people whose working lives are influenced by this individual. Find out more about the person from his or her boss. Find out what he or she is like to work with from other team members and co-workers. And find out what this person is like from the customer viewpoint. (It doesn't matter whether or not the individual has a traditional customer-facing job; everyone has customers of one sort or another.)

This should not be done sneakily. There is no intention to go behind the candidate's back. Any attempt to do so would have disastrous effects if the candidate subsequently found out. The idea, rather, is to find out more about the real life person, beyond the artificial picture painted by an application form and CV. The chances are there will be some variance. This doesn't mean for sure that the external view is right and the application is a whitewash – but whatever the reason, different perceptions matter, and other people will have to work with this individual in his or her new job.

The intention of this exercise is not to weed out difficult employees, but it can have such a side effect. If a manager finds out that one of his or her staff who has caused real problems has applied for another job, it's quite possible that the difficulties will be hushed up in the hope of getting rid of the individual. If the manager is asked outright, he or she is much less likely to lie; the truth will come out.

4

ENVIRONMENT CHECKLIST

WHY ENVIRONMENT?

Like the information available to you, the environment in which the interview takes place is a factor that you can influence before the interview in order to maximize the effectiveness of the time spent with the candidate. If you do nothing about the interview environment, perhaps thinking that it is none of your business, the interview might take place in an uncomfortable setting that does not bring out the best in the interviewee.

There is another important reason for considering the environment, too. There are elements that can be prepared in the environment that can make the experience of running the interview easier for you. This will help you to concentrate on your questions and the answers, rather than having your thoughts constantly flitting around environmental issues. Getting the environment right beforehand so you can relax and get on with the interview proper is an essential preparation.

This chapter consists of an environment checklist – a short list of environmental issues that you should check off before undertaking an interview – and some detail on each of these valuable items.

THE CHECKLIST

Appropriate office booked
Other locations considered
E-mail queries considered
Telephone interview considered
Mobile phone/pager switched off
No phone, or phone disconnected
Keep out signs
Chairs in position
Coffee table
Notepad
At least two pens
Clock in sight
Personal preparation
Dress
Hospitality

▌ *Appropriate office booked*

Your interviewees are likely to be on, what is to them, foreign territory. It won't help their confidence, nor will it encourage a sense of professionalism, if the room you use for the interview is inappropriate – for example, a windowless store cupboard half full of boxes with a couple of chairs hastily thrown in one corner. Nor will it look good if the interviewee turns up to find you arguing with the occupant of the room over bookings. Make sure you book an appropriate room, and turn up in plenty of time to be able to do something about it if anything is wrong.

Appropriate in this context means comfortably sized – not so small that those present invade each other's personal space, nor so huge that you seem to be a little island floating in space. It means private and free from distractions. An interviewee should not feel on display to the world during an interview, nor should he or she have a constant view of passers-by. If, as is the case in some modern buildings, all your meeting rooms and offices are glass walled, either make sure that the interviewee has his or her back to the glass, or go off-site for the interview. It is possible to screen glass using rolls of paper, but this usually looks amateurish and shabby.

▌ *Other locations considered*

It may be, as described in the previous category, that your available office space and meeting rooms are simply unsuitable for the job. It may be that you need to interview away from your company's building – anything from on-site at a university to a city centre recruitment fair. It may be that you simply want a change. Whatever the reason, it can be valuable to consider other locations than an office or meeting room in the building you work in.

There are a number of criteria to consider when making such a decision. Is the location easily accessible for the interviewee? Does it give the right impression about your company? Is it a cost-effective solution? In many cases an interview on your premises will be the best solution, but it makes sense to consider the alternatives, however briefly, and to check them off.

Note, by the way, that though alternative locations can be more interesting they do lack one benefit, as they fail to give the applicant a clear picture of the working ambience of the company and the area he or she is hoping to work in. This needs to be consciously countered, perhaps by providing a tour of the working environment and conversations with would-be co-workers to make up for the remote location of the interview.

▌ *E-mail queries considered*

While there is no substitute for a face-to-face interview, there are circumstances where you may wish to use alternative means to gather information. In a purely information gathering interview, the whole exercise could be undertaken using an exchange of e-mails, but for job or promotion interviewing, e-mail is not an appropriate main vehicle. However, it is very effective for providing the interviewee with information before the interview itself and for asking any simple, factual questions for which information has not already been supplied. Don't be afraid to make good use of this excellent resource when the need arises. E-mail can be particularly effective with an interviewee who is not regularly available on the telephone, as your electronic conversation is timed to suit the availability of the recipient rather than depending on the timings of the originator.

▮ Telephone interview considered

As with e-mail, the telephone is less than ideal as a vehicle for anything other than a basic fact-finding interview, but can prove an effective precursor to a job interview. Some companies make wide use of a telephone interview for an initial filtering interview. This is a doubtful practice unless telephone skills are a major part of the job, as few people are entirely natural on the telephone. A telephone interview also cripples the interviewer as all the body language is lost. Apart from as a source of basic information, it should be seen as a last resort when, for whatever reason, it is not possible to get together physically. Even so, the medium should be considered as part of your environmental checklist, if only in the form of a courtesy call to make sure that everything will be okay on the day.

Unlike e-mail, a telephone interview is thrust upon the interviewee. It is highly unlikely that he or she will have been sitting by the phone waiting for your call, and so the interviewee will typically be in the middle of another task if you make an unexpected call. For this reason, it should be entirely acceptable (in fact, you should suggest) at the start of an unplanned interview call for the interviewee to ask to be called back in a few minutes time, to enable him or her to pull together the essential requirements for the interview. Better, though, is to schedule the interview in the first place.

▮ Mobile phone/pager switched off

It's common practice these days for cinemas to show warnings before the film to remind the public to switch off any mobile phones so that the film isn't disturbed by a succession of rings, chirps and loud tunes. A mobile phone that rings is an immediate and unfair distraction for the interviewee. Make sure before starting that your phone is switched off. Remember, too, any pagers and other mobile devices such as personal organizers and alarm watches that may produce a distraction.

If you forget to turn your phone off (it happens to the best of us) and it does ring, whatever you do, resist the temptation to answer it. This sends a very clear signal to the interviewee. Your call is more important than they are. You aren't really interested in what they have to say. They might as well go home now. Apologize to the interviewee, then, if your phone supports it, divert the call directly to your voice mail and switch off. If it doesn't, switch straight off, whoever is calling. There should be no exceptions to this.

▎ *No phone, or phone disconnected*

Mobiles aren't the only potential source of distraction. A conventional phone can be just as irritating. If you are operating from your own office, make sure that you have diverted your phone elsewhere. Don't just switch on voicemail or an answering machine where the phone still rings, but is answered after a while; the ringing is enough to be a distraction even if you don't answer the phone. If the room is strange to you, make sure you search it before the interview begins. It's not uncommon for an infrequently used office to have a phone tucked away in a corner, perhaps on the floor. If it happens to ring, you'll not only have to answer it, but play 'hunt the phone', which doesn't look at all professional. Ensure any phones that can't be redirected are disconnected, even if it means pulling the wire out of the wall.

▎ *Keep out signs*

Although the telephone is the most common form of interruption, it's not unheard of for someone to wander into a room in the middle of an interview. This causes confusion, lots of distraction and everyone is highly embarrassed. Worst of all, some people won't recognize the sacrosanct nature of the interview and will try to hold a conversation with you because 'it's something quick' or 'it's urgent.'

It is important that you do your best to prevent such incursions. A large sign reading something like 'Interview in progress: please do not enter' will put off the majority of would-be irritants. It's even better if you can have someone stationed in an outer office to fend off even those who feel that their need is greater than the requirement to avoid disturbing the interview. This can also be helpful if you have a string of interviews, as the next candidate, turning up to find a door with such a notice, can never be sure whether to go straight in, or wait for the previous person to come out (if there was such a person).

▎ *Chairs in position*

The vast majority of interviews are conducted sitting down, which means having appropriate chairs for all those involved, ready and in position (see comments below on having a clock in sight). The interviewee's chair should be so positioned that it is reasonably obvious which it is (although do indicate this as he or she comes in, too – don't leave the interviewee wondering where to go). However, clear positioning doesn't mean that the set up has to be confrontational. If, for instance, you have three interviewers to one interviewee, you can position the interviewers' chairs in an arc, to make the interviewee's position feel more included.

Chairs could be of any kind, but make sure both the interviewers' and interviewee's are of a similar type. Armchairs are fine in a setting like a hotel lounge, but in an office setting it is probably best to stick with the more comfortable style of office chair. Think twice about having chairs that swivel or rock – you may find it difficult not to do this, and it can be distracting. The chairs should be in a group, but not so close that there is any danger of knee contact. Consider the coffee table (see next section) as a natural spacer.

▌ Coffee table

Interviewing across a desk or a meeting table is overly distancing. It makes the relationship very clearly 'them and us' and can be intimidating, especially if there are several interviewers. It is much better to do away with such a heavy-duty barrier. But to have nothing at all is equally likely to be uncomfortable. The best compromise seems to be to have a coffee table, which doesn't act as a barrier, but is enough of a spacer to feel that you aren't being confrontational or overly familiar. It is also handy if you want to put down any documents like an application form, or a drink.

▌ Notepad

It is inevitable that you will need something to make notes on. It simply isn't practical to keep all the details of an interview in your head – let alone a whole series of interviews. In principle, you could keep your notes on a laptop computer or palmtop, but it is particularly distracting for the interviewee and it's not easy to make the notes without concentrating too much on the screen and keyboard. For all its low-tech connotations, pen and paper still works best. Assuming you are working from a chair with a coffee table in front of you, it's not practical to lean on the table to write, so it is probably best to use a clipboard. They look rather officious, but they are very practical.

▌ At least two pens

There's an element of the scout or guide about the good interviewer – always prepared for something to go wrong. If you only bother to take one pen to the interview, it's somehow inevitable that it will dry up and you will have to borrow another pen from an interviewer, or even worse from the interviewee. Note that the second pen is purely there as a standby. Interviewing is not a good time to employ a note-taking technique that uses all sorts of coloured pens for different types of note. The interviewee is liable to be so mesmerized with your pen swapping that he or she forgets to answer your questions.

▌ Clock in sight

Time is a strange thing in interviews. It can run away, or drag on forever. Usually an interview has to fit within a schedule, so you need to keep track of time and be prepared to move the candidate on if it looks like you aren't going to get through all your key questions. Unfortunately, there is an inescapable interpretation of looking at your watch. It is seen as being critical, suggesting someone should get a move on, or that the interview is simply boring.

If possible, arrange the interview room with a clock on the wall behind the interviewee. This means that you can glance at the time whenever you like without being seen to take your eyes far off the interviewee. It also means that the interviewee isn't tempted to clock-watch, which could damage his or her performance. If this isn't possible (be prepared to rearrange the furniture to put any clock in the room behind the interviewee), you will need to employ the surreptitious watch glance. Get your watch out from under your cuff (if there is one) without looking at it at all. Still looking at the candidate, position your watch so that it would be in clear view if you glanced down. Then at an appropriate moment, look at your notes or look down briefly as if in thought, taking in the time from your watch incidentally.

▌ Personal preparation

If you are engaged in a whole sequence of interviews, you may find it particularly difficult to fit in any time for attention to your personal needs. Don't let a tight schedule take over, though. Ensure that you have at least 5 to 10 minutes between interviews to finish any last minute notes, to make sure you are on top of the next interviewee's details and cope with any personal requirements. You need to be comfortable – if you have been sitting with your legs crossed for an hour waiting to go to the loo you are unlikely to give your best. Spend a moment checking your grooming (hair, dandruff on clothes, straight tie/skirt and so on). If necessary, take a quick snack and drink to keep yourself performing well. It is quite acceptable to still be drinking when the interviewee comes in (at least, if you are going to offer interviewees something themselves), but don't let it get in the way – ignore it and let it get cold if your concentration requires it. For some reason, it is not acceptable to eat once the interviewee is present – just don't do it; the image you will give will be unprofessional.

▌ Dress

Bearing in mind that the interviewee may be entering foreign territory, it is worth being specific about the dress required for the interview. While it's interesting to see what an interviewee would choose, it can be unfortunate if a candidate totally misjudges the situation. This can happen to anyone, as in the example already cited of the 1990s meeting between IBM and Apple Computer where the IBM executives turned up in jeans and T-shirt to match the recognized Apple look, and the Apple executives turned up in suits. This bilateral attempt came out positively just because it was bilateral. As only the interviewee has the possibility of getting it wrong, you shouldn't leave it to chance.

If you do specify how the interviewee should dress, ideally you should dress in a similar way. If, for instance, you specify casual clothes but turn up yourself in a business suit, the interviewee may feel disadvantaged.

▌ Hospitality

The degree of hospitality offered to the interviewee will depend on the scale of the interviews and the distance the interviewee has come. If you are expecting the interviewee to be present across (say) breakfast or lunch it would be polite to provide the appropriate meal. If there's a chance for the interviewees to have the meal informally with someone from your company (ideally not the interviewers), this is a good opportunity to get a feel for what the interviewees are really like – and for them to get a better picture of the company.

If you intend to have a drink during an interview, don't do so and totally ignore the interviewee, who may have had to leave home early and not have had a cup of tea or coffee. Offering a drink at the start of an interview can be a good way to break down barriers, provided there is something to put the drink on, like a coffee table. Don't offer a drink part way through the interview, though, as it will break the flow.

5

SELLING CHECKLIST

WHY SELLING?

It's very rare that an interview doesn't involve a degree of selling. Unless your company and your job are simply the best possible options on the market and nothing else comes close, you will be in the position where your most favoured applicants have a choice. Not only will you want them, so will other companies. So part of the role of the interview will be to sell your company and your job to the applicant: to explain why he or she should want this job over and above any other (although avoid getting into this literal position, if possible); to emphasize all the advantages and opportunities that arise from coming to work for you. Inevitably there is a balance here. You can't offer so much that it ceases to be cost effective to make a job offer – but you need to offer something.

At first sight this might seem to imply that you have to be soft, that you are going to roll over and let the applicants walk all over you. But it's not like that. Your interview can be as intense and probing as you like. Towards the end, though, you need to change tack a little. Ask the interviewee if there's anything they would like to ask about the company and the job. And whether or not they do, give the applicant a short sales pitch. Send him or her out on a high, inspired by the thought of coming to work for your company. This won't be the case for every single interview. With some candidates, you know all too well by the end that there isn't the slightest hope that this applicant will get a job offer, in which case limit yourself to asking if they have any questions. But otherwise, if there's a chance of making an offer, sell.

In an internal interview it will obviously be unnecessary to sell many of the features of working in this company, but there will still be opportunities for stressing some of the selling points – anything from flexibility of working to career opportunities. Even in a performance review interview (at least for a good candidate), you will want to sell, to keep the individual in the company, and ideally in your part of the company.

This chapter consists of a selling checklist – a short list of sales issues that you should check off before undertaking an interview – and some detail on each of the selling items.

THE CHECKLIST

Company brochures
Details of the package
Flexible working options
Dress
Support options
The office space
Food and drink
Car parking and public transport
Details of social facilities
Tools for the job
Opportunities for advancement
Career flexibility
Training
Travel
Perks
Migration support
A visit

▌ Company brochures

Many large companies produce brochures especially intended to entice new recruits. Others may have general brochures about the company itself. Do give these as part of the selling process, but only as the interview closes, so the brochure does not become a distraction that breaks up the conversation. Brochures by themselves won't do too much, but they will help to set the image, and give a candidate who has travelled by public transport something to read on the way home.

▌ Details of the package

The most basic selling has to be around the contents of the package you are offering. The pay, any bonus schemes and incentives, performance related pay, leave entitlement and similar facts. Setting these levels isn't part of the interview process, but getting them right is essential if you intend to get the level of employee you desire. If possible, use one of the agencies (Hay MSL, for example) that provide tables of salary levels for various types of jobs so you can pitch your rewards effectively.

If you know that your salaries are, say, around the 75th percentile, make something of it. Point out that your salaries are in the top 25 per cent of similar employers, and though some will offer more, your package provides greater opportunities for advancement (you can't have any evidence for this, but it's a good general statement). If you have performance related pay, bonus schemes and stock options, make a big thing of them. It's very difficult to make a straight comparison, and if you emphasize how much a top performer can get it is very impressive. If you don't have performance related pay, bonus schemes and stock options, get them. It's time you dragged the company into the 21st century. Make sure, also, that the advantages of good performance are significant – performance related pay that only dabbles with a few per cent provides very little incentive. Chunky performance pay, perhaps 20 per cent or more, is much more effective both as a way of attracting candidates and of retaining and giving an incentive to good staff.

▌ Flexible working options

The days are long gone when every employee wants and expects a contract that specifies they will work Monday to Friday, 9.00 am–5.30 pm (though realizing that the company really expects them to work at least 60 hours a week). Flexibility is increasingly attractive to many employees. The more you can offer, the better your chances of capturing the cream of the applicants.

Apart from the opportunities of using part-time working, flexitime is the simplest option. Allowing the individual to select when they work their hours gives them the ability to avoid traffic congestion or deal with a specific personal requirement. Many schemes provide flexidays where the staff member can work extra hours, then use up these banked hours to take extra leave. Most schemes use a core hour concept of certain hours when the individual has to be present, although this is not essential.

Flexibility is not just about time, though. The percentage of people working from home is on the increase. If you can offer the option of working part of the week from home, you will attract many individuals who don't appreciate the daily commute and find that they are much more productive in a home office. Homeworking has a cost – providing the home equipment, insurance and so on – but this can be offset against expensive office accommodation if home working results in a reduction of space required. To reduce costs may imply having hot-desking in the office. While some jobs can't be run from home, a lot more can than are currently allowed for, especially with modern high-speed computer links like ISDN and ADSL. For some, the home office can be full time, only coming into the office for meetings. For others, one or two days a week might be regularly in the main office – but the benefits are significant both for the company and for the individual.

Forcing homeworking on anyone will inevitably have a negative effect, but having it on offer will make your company more attractive for very many employees. Don't dismiss the possibility.

▎ *Dress*

At one time it was entirely accepted that the employees wore a uniform, whether it was a specifically patterned apron or boiler suit, or the uniformity of the business suit. It can still be advantageous for customer-facing staff to wear uniforms, but for back-office staff, the time is coming to move away from uncomfortable uniformity. In the UK, as a result of 'dress-down Fridays' and similar initiatives, a number of highly respected institutions have already got rid of the suit and tie (or female equivalent). In the US, respected high technology firms have rarely insisted on formal dress, and the approach is spreading even faster. If you are recruiting staff born since the 1950s, the chances are that you will appeal more if you have a back-office policy of casual clothes being acceptable.

▎ *Support options*

At various points in a career, an individual will have need for support. It might be due to sickness or having children. It might be when buying a house or suffering bereavement. Many of these occasions have statutory requirements, but these are the minimum you can offer. If your company can show that it has consideration for the workforce by offering, say, more than the statutory paternity leave or by giving some form of assistance to first-time house buyers, it is going to be an excellent selling point.

▎ *The office space*

For many staff, the office represents a space in which they will spend a lot of time (subject to the comments above about homeworking). Using the office itself to sell the job has two aspects. The first centres around the nature of the provision. What will the individual's personal space be like? How will it be decorated? What furniture will they have? Will there be a window? Is it open-plan or in individual offices?

The second aspect of the office space is the flexibility of personalization. How much can the individual make the space their own? Some large offices have draconian limitations – nothing stuck on walls, no changes to standard furniture, and so on. This is with the intention of providing a 'neat' uniform designer look. But it also prevents the individuals who work there from making the space feel comfortable. You need to decide which is more important, and if you can be flexible, point this out.

▎ Food and drink

Unless yours is a virtual organization, your employees spend a significant proportion of their lives in and around your premises. The facilities that are provided on site will make a difference to the attractiveness of the prospect. Take, for example, the British Airways headquarters building, Waterside. This has a glassed-over street with pavement cafés, a small branch of the supermarket Waitrose (employees can place an order from their desktop to be picked up after work), a bank and various market-style stalls. There are several restaurants with different levels of formality. And each open-plan office section has a drinks machine with free drinks for employees. Other companies, Microsoft for example, provide canned drinks (sodas) free for employees.

If you have older premises, or your company is too small to provide cafés and other features, find out as much as you can about the surroundings. Are you based on a high street with a couple of excellent cafés and bars? Emphasize their availability. Perhaps you could arrange for sandwich companies or pizza firms to deliver, or for local restaurants to offer a discount to your staff. With a little imagination, you can still make the eating and drinking facilities a selling point.

▎ Car parking and public transport

Getting to work these days can be fraught with problems. It's one of the reasons for the increasing popularity of homeworking. Anything that you can offer to support your end of the transport problem can make a big difference. Many offices were not designed with enough car parking. If you can guarantee a parking space for those who are driving to work, you will seem more attractive than the sort of employer where anyone arriving after 8.30 am has to take their luck on nearby side-streets (and faces the wrath of the occupants).

For the many people who prefer to come to work by public transport, any accessibility you have is worth selling. Are you near a station or bus stop? Do you know the frequencies of the trains or buses, and where they come from? Large companies might consider negotiating with bus companies to site a stop, or laying on public transport to key locations where it isn't already available.

▌ Details of social facilities

Making it possible to eat and drink at work is an essential, but the opportunities for becoming a more attractive employer through social facilities don't stop there. Many large companies have a wide range of social clubs, some offering subsidies to support clubs and facilities. If you have, make sure you emphasize the benefits of these. If you don't, look for ways you can work with existing sports and social facilities. For instance, could you get a special deal with the local swimming pool or bar?

▌ Tools for the job

Where the job involves the use of equipment, the quality of that equipment can be an influencing factor in choosing to work for your company. Computer programmers, for example, like to work with the latest, fastest machines, and to know that they will be upgraded on a very regular basis. Depending on your business, you might provide mobile phones, cars, laptop computers, engineering machinery – a whole range of equipment. If you can emphasize the value of these to the individual, and that you are using the latest, top-of-the-range devices, you can give yourself the edge over a competitor that thrashes every last ounce of effort out of its machinery and begrudges employees the tools they need for the job.

It's important with this one (and in fact the rest of your sales pitch) that you deliver on the promise. It's easy if you don't know much about it to believe that you do, for instance, provide the latest PCs, only to discover that your new, whiz-kid programmer thinks what she gets is out of the ark. This will not go down well.

▌ Opportunities for advancement

If you are recruiting someone to stay with the company for a fair while, he or she will probably not expect to stay in the same job for the whole time. If you can show clear opportunities for promotion without waiting for the previous occupants of jobs to move on, you will seem more attractive than a company that is obviously moribund. More junior staff may appreciate having a well mapped-out career path, although senior recruits may prefer to know of a wide range of opportunities, but will want to take charge of their own progression.

▌ Career flexibility

Related to advancement, but subtly different, is the opportunity for career flexibility. If yours is a large company, you may be able to offer a wide range of career paths, leading into totally different parts of the organization. Someone might, for example, join in a human relations role and end up managing a marketing group. The more you can offer this sort of flexibility and range of opportunity, the more attractive your company will seem for long-term employment.

It's also worth looking at a different aspect of career flexibility, too. Can you offer some form of career breaks? Could an individual take a year off to do something completely different? Sabbaticals in business are growing in popularity – if you can offer them, you will improve your position, particularly with more senior recruits.

▌ Training

Opportunities for training should be highlighted. This is particularly the case with developmental training. If you have a target for number of days of training a year or a budget allocation per head (and it isn't embarrassingly low), make something of it. Run through how an individual will be trained for the job (if necessary), what facilities are possible for advancement and what in-service qualifications can be gained. You may, for example, offer your junior managers the chance to work for an MBA. At a senior level, you could also look at paid study leave to attend a high-level management college such as the Harvard Business School.

In many areas of business there are conferences where an employee can meet with like-minded individuals, both to learn from the seminars and workshops and to share experience. Offering the ability to attend appropriate conferences can be a very attractive part of the training sales pitch. The fact that such conferences are often in desirable locations around the world can also be encouraging for the would-be employee.

▌ Travel

For many people, travel is an enjoyable part of the job. Having established this is the case with the particular applicant (not everyone does enjoy travel), go into the travel opportunities that will go along with the job. If you offer more than average travelling support (first class rail travel or business class air travel, for example), let the applicant know. If the travel involves exotic locations, emphasize how easy it is to take a few extra days on site as leave, thus getting free travel to a desirable destination.

▌ Perks

Many companies have opportunities for the employees that are described by the rather derogatory term 'perks'. These are benefits that the general public do not receive that the employee can have as a result of his or her position. Perks can be generic, like private medical cover, a company car or a clothes allowance, or can be specific to the company. Usually the latter involves cheaper access to the company's products or services than is available to the normal customers.

Wherever possible, offer these specific perks at near cost, so the employee really feels the benefit. This can result in real bargains where the variable cost of an additional product is very low – for example, in standby seats on aircraft. You should also consider how far you can extend your perks beyond the individual employee. Some companies include close family. Others have an extension of the scheme where the employee can provide the products or services to anyone they like at a lesser discount.

In effect, the employee is acting as an agent. Everyone gains from such a system, so it is foolish not to have it.

▌ Migration support

Moving to a new job is not always a simple matter of changing employer. It might mean moving house, with all the hassle that is associated with this. It could even mean temporarily or permanently changing country of residence. The more support you can offer to make this migration painless for the employee, the more attractive you will seem. You might, for instance, pay for a hotel or rented accommodation until a house is bought. You might support a bridging loan, pay removal expenses and legal fees. You might take away the fiddly details of getting a work permit or sending out change of address notification. The easier you can make it for someone to come to your company, the more attractive you will seem.

▌ A visit

Assuming your workplace is an attractive place to be, arranging a visit can be a helpful selling tactic. It's a subtle version of the oldest trick in the book. If a salesman can actually put the product in front of the would-be customer and say, 'You can have it now, right away', he or she is more likely to get a sale than if the customer has to wait a month to get the goods. It's childish, but it is true – seeing the goods in front of you does make them more attractive to buy.

You can do something similar by arranging a workplace tour as part of the interview process. What you are saying is, 'All this could be yours'. It gives the potential employee a chance to talk to the people they will be working with, to really get a feel for the advantages of the position you have on offer.

Of course, there's a risk. The workplace might not seem attractive to the applicant. The other workers may actively discourage the applicant from coming to this company. But if that's the case, you've got problems that hiring a new staff member isn't going to cure.

6

QUESTION FILE

ABOUT QUESTIONS

Questions are the meat and drink of the interview. Your skill in asking the right questions in the right way can make all the difference. We have already looked at the importance of using open questions. Your aim is to probe the interviewee's thoughts and experience. The more they open up and talk, the more likely you are to achieve this. Most people enjoy talking about themselves – if you make them comfortable in an interview, your questions become simple pointers to the right direction and the information comes out.

In this chapter there are 100 sample questions. There is no suggestion that you limit yourself to these – they are just examples of effective questions and the sort of response each question might elicit. Feel free to use actual questions from the list, but in many cases it will be more effective to use them as guides and to develop your own questions that fit best with your personal style. You should never seem to be reading questions – at that point an interview ceases to be a conversation. Make sure that a number of your questions flow from what has already been said, and that the questions you prepare are written down in keyword form, so the phrasing you use is natural and on the spur of the moment, rather than stilted reading from a script.

SELECTING FROM THE MENU

In choosing the questions you are to use, consider the flow of the interview. Have a specific opening question prepared, which should be gentle, warm and encouraging. From there on you will need to play the progress of the interview by ear. If the interviewee makes a comment that needs expanding on, take that expansion first. If his or her response naturally chains into other questions, head off in that direction. You should have in keyword form all the questions you need to ask to get the information you require, plus half a dozen general questions that can be used as fillers if nothing arises out of the interviewee's comments.

Have an expected order in which you intend to ask the questions, but be prepared to let this go to follow a natural conversational flow. It may even be that the opening question never gets asked because the interviewee launches into a conversational gambit before you have a chance to ask it. That's fine – don't fight it, go with the flow.

I would strongly recommend having your prepared questions in some mind mapped or similar form (see exercise 2.9). That way you can skip around the questions, choosing the most appropriate, depending on the context. You can also attach your notes of the responses to the questions. I have found that the best approach in interviews is to use one of the alternative concept mapping approaches which, unlike a mind map, does not have a single central point, but perhaps half a dozen separate centres on the page, with different topics, each having questions branching out from it. This makes it easier to navigate with the limited attention you can give your notes during the interview.

MANAGING THE FLOW

An experienced interviewee will get the message he or she wants to put across whatever you ask – here your efforts have to make sure that the questions you want answered get dealt with, as well as those that fulfil the interviewee's goals. You can hear this happening whenever a politician is interviewed on TV or radio. Whatever question the interviewer asks, experienced politicians will steer the conversation round to the subject they want to talk about. The good interviewer will give them a short opportunity to get their message across, then come back to the original question. This can take a lot of persistence, as demonstrated by UK television interviewer Jeremy Paxman, who once asked a minister the same question over 20 times in an attempt to get a straight answer.

GENERAL PERSONALITY QUESTIONS

Some of the questions in this section will help to get the interview off to a comfortable start; others are designed to probe the personality of the interviewee in a general way.

1. *What do you think you will bring to the job?*

    A double question as it asks interviewees both what they think the job requires, and what they can do to satisfy that requirement. The interviewee has to tread the fine line between modesty and boastfulness, which can provide useful insights into his or her interpersonal skills.

2. *Why did you choose your university/college?*

    If you are interviewing graduates, this question manages to be both an introduction and quite penetrating. Be suspicious of anyone who comes up with too reasoned an argument – most teenagers aren't that structured and he or she is probably enhancing the truth. A better candidate would be honest in saying that they didn't put enough effort into the choice at the time, but they would have chosen it now because... and then comes the reasoning.

3. *What was the best thing about your previous job (or college/university/school or holiday job)... and what was the worst?*

    The second half of this two-part question can be quite tricky for the interviewee. Don't let him or her escape into saying there was nothing bad. All things are relative, and some must have been worse than others. Look out for answers that show a bad fit with the nature of the job that the interviewee is applying for.

4. *What is your greatest strength?*

    Another testing question for the individual. Look out for (and if necessary probe for) a specific example of this strength being applied, rather than a general assertion. Obviously the strength should be aligned to the job requirements.

5. *And your greatest weakness?*

    It's always worth throwing this one in as well. Despite any preparation they may have had, this is always a tricky one for the interviewee. Be wary of a candidate who can't identify any weaknesses – or has too many. Look for a weakness that has positive attributes as far as the job you are interviewing for is concerned.

6. *Describe a difficult situation you have had to handle.*

Look for the way the candidate assessed the situation, making sure that he or she understood just what it was, developed one or more solutions, selected an appropriate approach (if there were several solutions) and planned and executed the implementation. Also look for an understanding of why the situation was difficult.

7. *Why have you chosen to apply to this company?*

An element of business awareness here, but a lot of it is about the candidate themselves. Look for good preparation, and be prepared to go into a bit more depth if you get general remarks like, 'It is a large, well-respected company.' Why is it well respected? Why does that make it worth applying to? Why does that appeal to this individual?

8. *How would you describe yourself?*

Not an intensely valuable question in content, but it's a useful 'breather' question if you need a chance to regroup, and it may reveal something of the candidate's self-image.

9. *How would your current boss/tutor describe you?*

Useful either alone or in conjunction with the previous question. You may get a more honest answer from this 'outside view' question. There will probably be a need to push through an initial, vague reply (eg 'generally effective, I think') to get to more detail.

10. *Have you any questions?*

A useful closing question, which makes it feel as if the interview is over, but it isn't. If the candidate has no questions, they are poorly prepared or indifferent. Look for questions with a degree of insight and openness. Don't be put off because a question is hard for you to answer – and that includes questions about you, the interviewer, as an employee.

SKILLS QUESTIONS

An important part of an interview is to understand what the interviewee is capable of. Some jobs will involve very specific skills, and there will be a need to probe these, but these general questions will stand you in good stead with most interviewees.

1. *What do you see the responsibilities of a X as?*

    In the question, X is the job the interviewee is applying for. The applicant should have a reasonable idea of the requirements of the job and, just as importantly, how that job will involve interacting with different parts of the organization. Don't expect too much precision though – the same job will mean very different things in different companies; you can't expect an interviewee to know too much about 'the way we do things round here'.

2. *Which aspects of this job do you think are most important?*

    It's all very well to have nominal skills for the job, but any post will have different priorities and an understanding of these is crucial to being able to do the job properly.

3. *Which areas of the job do you consider you are most skilled at?*

    This question looks into the candidate's perception of their skills, and how they apply. Correlate the response to both the job description and the other information you have about the candidate, and be prepared to reflect what you discover back to the candidate.

4. *What basis do you have for this assertion?*

    Be prepared to ask for a justification of the interviewee's claims, even if it feels a little cruel. If he or she has already given examples and justification, there is no need for this question, but don't take a straight statement without some corroboration.

5. *What would your first steps be in training someone else for this job?*

    A rather different and often valuable way of getting a feel for the candidate's understanding of the job. It also takes the pressure off slightly, as it feels like the candidate is 'one of us'.

6. *What skills do you have that don't form part of the job description, but would still be valuable here?*

    Sometimes it's the tangential skills that are most important. Often, for instance, a job will require better communications skills than is obvious from a job description. See how the candidate responds to this proposition.

7. *If you were working with a small team of other people, what skills would you consider complimentary to your own?*

    A slightly devious way of asking what skills the candidate is lacking in, but the question also examines his or her understanding of group working.

8. *How do you make sure you get tasks completed on time?*

    This question looks at time management skills, which are liable to be important in practically any job. It should particularly bring out his or her attitude to finishing (rather than doing).

9. *What environment do you prefer to work in?*

    An element of teamwork and manageability here, but this question is also looking for how the candidate's skills fit with the working environment, whether they would be suited to teleworking, and so on. You may need to clarify what you mean by 'environment'.

10. *Which are you more confident with, written or verbal communications, and why?*

    Communications skills in some form will be valuable in practically any job. This question looks at these skills, and may reveal something of the candidate's weaknesses when the comparison is made.

BUSINESS AWARENESS QUESTIONS

It is rarely the case now that a candidate can get away with knowing all there is to know about his or her job, but being in a state of sublime ignorance about the business. This is an inevitable conclusion of the move to giving staff more flexibility and responsibility in order to cope with the fast-changing world they face. Flexibility implies being guided by principles and understanding, not just following a set of rules. And an understanding of how the role fits in the business and what the business is all about is essential to set the context of those principles.

1. *Why do you think you would like this job?*

    A deceptively simple question that probes the interviewee's preparation for the interview. You are not only asking him or her for their match to the job, but also what they know about the role.

2. *Tell me a bit about this company.*

    You can't expect the interviewee to have an insider's insight, but you can expect them to have researched the company and know the highlights of your business. Look for understanding beyond simply repeating what is easily found on your Web site. Be prepared here, though. The more astute interviewee, having given a good answer, might finish with 'but of course, I'm seeing it from the outside – what do you think I've missed?' and put you on the spot, so do your homework, too.

3. *How does this job relate to the department and the company's goals?*

    Like all good questions, this has complex intent. You are looking for both an understanding of the nature of the job they are applying for, the role of the department and overall goals of the company.

4. *What business do you think this company is in?*

    This question encourages the interviewee to think a little about the realities of business. The more perceptive candidates may see beyond the simple label ('it's an airline', 'it's a publisher') and bring out the realities of the business ('We're about getting people where they want to go', 'We fulfil dreams', 'We package expertise'). Don't worry, though, if there isn't a neat phrase like this, as long as the candidate sees beyond the basics.

5. *Who are our main competitors?*

    If the interviewee knows something about the company, he or she should also have some idea of whom the company's competitors are. The response here will reflect the individual's preparedness and ability to undertake research.

6. *Who are our main competitors likely to be in five years' time, and why?*

A much more searching question than the previous one. This question expects the candidate to really think about the world in which the business operates. It doesn't matter if the answer is the one your strategists would give – the important thing is that the candidate thinks outside the predictable competitors of today in new and innovative directions.

7. *How do you think our company compares with our competitors?*

An extension to question 5, the candidate not only has to know something about the company and its competitors, but also about the criteria by which such businesses can be rated and compared.

8. *What do you think are our top three costs?*

A nitty-gritty examination of the candidate's gut feel for one of the prime business drivers. It doesn't matter whether or not the answer is 100 per cent right, as long as it is logical and well thought out.

9. *Give me a picture of our most important customers.*

This could either be literal (ie who the most important customers are) or a more general description of the type of customer that is liable to be important to the company. Part of the value of the question is seeing how the candidate deals with the key word 'important'.

10. *What could we do to improve our revenue?*

Again a very open question that gives the candidate an opportunity to display his or her understanding of the company, how it does business and what chances there are to improve it.

TEAMWORK QUESTIONS

The ability to work well with others is a requirement in practically any job. Even an apparently stand-alone task, like writing a book, will involve interaction with a wide range of other people to ensure successful completion. Probing the candidate's attitude to teamwork involves getting a clear picture of his or her understanding of how teams work, and which of the potential team roles he or she fits best in. Questions on motivating a team appear in the leadership section below.

1. *How do you get on with working with others?*

   Only the most naïve of interviewees is going to own up to being incapable of teamwork, but there is an opportunity here to probe exactly how the individual copes.

2. *Can you describe circumstances when you work best alone, and when you work best in a team?*

   Expand on this if necessary to explore the individual's understanding of teamwork. If they are simply trying to follow the party line that 'team is best' they will have difficulty coming up with both examples – if they understand the reality better, they will realize that some tasks need solo concentration while others benefit hugely from being part of a team.

3. *What are your pet hates at work?*

   This question could appear in almost any section; I've put it in teamwork because the answer is often oriented to other people. Don't let the interviewee get away with, 'I haven't got any' – come back with, 'There must be something, it's only human', or something similar. Obvious doubtful replies are those about pretty normal behaviour for co-workers or customers. Look for a response that identifies something that will tend to mess up the business, tied with an understanding of the cause so that the interviewee would react coolly rather than emotionally.

4. *How do you feel about sports?*

   I've partly included this question as it is often misused. There is a feeling that someone who plays a team sport is more of a team player, hence a better choice. Unfortunately, not only are many team sport players very poor at teamwork in practice, but they are also less liable to show initiative than, say, a player of a more strategic game. However, it's worth asking the question to distinguish between those who enjoy watching and those who enjoy taking part. Someone who enjoys playing badminton is a more likely bet than someone who thinks watching a team game like football is a great pastime.

5. *What role do you tend to take in a team?*

   Check out the candidate's understanding of teams and his or her preferred role. Practically everyone has a preferred role, so if he or she says they don't, you ought to be suspicious. It may be, though, that he or she doesn't understand the concept of roles in a team. If necessary, probe by discussing different team roles.

6. *What makes a good team?*

   Again, this is looking at an understanding of teams. Look for something more than 'the members work well together'. Concepts like synergy, the complimentary nature of differing roles and so on should be present.

7. *Give an example of when you were involved in a great team, and describe why it was great.*

   A useful expansion on the previous question if you suspect the answer was based more on book theory than on practical experience. Almost everyone should have some example of good teamwork, even if it was in an unimportant context. Make sure you get the 'why' as well as the 'what'.

8. *Why is teamwork important in this job/department/company?*

   See how well the interviewee can translate a theoretical knowledge of the value of teamworking into a specific analysis of the requirements in this job or company. It's very unlikely that the answer should be 'it isn't.'

9. *Why do some teams fail?*

   Again, this is looking for a good understanding of the way people work together. This is an interesting question, because you can understand how things ought to be without knowing the realities of how things fall apart. Ask for specific examples (whether or not the candidate was part of the team in question).

10. *How do you get on with different kinds of people?*

    If you get generalities, make sure that he or she comes up with one or two concrete examples. As with most of the team questions, the aim is to probe the candidate's understanding of teams and how they fit in with the types of people they may have to work with.

LEADERSHIP QUESTIONS

The leadership questions span both leadership and motivation; even if the candidate isn't applying for a management position, there may well be opportunities for motivating others. Considerable stress is put here on the distinction between old-fashioned management and the sort of leadership that is necessary to cope with the modern business environment. A secondary role of this section is making the distinction between leadership and arrogance.

1. *What is the difference between a leader and a manager?*

   This distinction is increasingly important. A manager provides his or her staff with a clear set of tasks, then monitors the execution of those tasks. A leader sets clear principles and directions, then lets the individual get on with the execution, providing support rather than monitoring how the tasks are completed. Management makes sense in inflexible situations, where there is little change. Leadership makes sense when the world is constantly changing and the staff members need to react appropriately, rather than follow set rules. Accordingly, leadership tends to be more appropriate in the modern business world.

2. *Would you say you had more leadership or management traits?*

   It is worth asking the previous question first, and the answer here will inevitably depend on the sort of answer already given. Expand it with, 'Why do you say that?' if the answer is too closed. Which traits you want depend on the job, but increasingly it is leadership that is required in a fast-changing, highly flexible business world.

3. *How do you feel about responsibility?*

   You are unlikely to be looking for power-hungry people, but rather for those who feel that their experience has shown that taking responsibility is something that they are good at, and enjoy the challenges of. Look for, and if necessary prompt for, a good example of taking responsibility.

4. *If you are in a room full of people with a group task to do and no one in charge, what is your response?*

   Be wary of the person who wades in and tries to take charge immediately. A good leader is more likely to try to bring everyone in, assess their potential contributions and encourage them into action – to take charge of the process rather than the people. Look for this in the response.

5. *Are you a natural leader?*

Look for someone who understands the personality traits that make a good leader, and says that they feel they are well endowed with these, but that there's always more to develop – anyone who is prepared to say outright that they are a great natural leader should be treated with suspicion. This is an intentionally closed question. It can be answered 'yes' or 'no' – but anyone who does so is not very good at communication. Use silence to get a response.

6. *If you had to lead highly technical staff, what would you use to establish your authority?*

This question reflects French and Raven's structure of power. Traditional management relies on three prime mechanisms: reward power (the ability to decide on reward levels), coercive power (the stick to accompany the carrot) and legitimate power (power vested by structure and tradition). Technical staff tend not to respect these power bases, being more driven by referent power (charismatic leadership) and expert power (based on real or perceived specialist knowledge). Your interviewee needn't know the details of this theory, but ought to be aware that technical people are much more likely to respond to a degree of expertise and charisma than they are to authority, threats or (to some degree) rewards.

7. *How would you influence people over whom you have no authority?*

You are looking here for an understanding of the common necessity in business to set a lead where there is no formal structure of power.

8. *Describe the time you acted best as a leader, in work or outside.*

This question might not be necessary as a result of developments from questions 3 or 4 (if used), but if the candidate hasn't come up with a good example, it's worth pushing for it to help to clarify his or her understanding of leadership.

9. *As a leader, how do you balance being a member of your team and also your peer group?*

There is always a balancing act being part of your own team and a management team or similar. The good leader has to see themselves as part of their own team – if his or her attitude is to think of the team as 'them' rather than 'us', he or she isn't a leader. Accordingly the leader has to see himself or herself as the team's representative on the management team. It doesn't mean that the local team is always put first, but this has to be the starting point.

10. *Should a leader be prepared to ask staff to do something he or she isn't prepared to do?*

Again an intentionally closed question, but any decent communicator can open it up and should. A slightly tricky one, this. The natural inclination is to say 'no', but in fact a leader won't have the same skills as staff and so inevitably will be asking staff to do things he or she can't do. However, leaders should also lead by example, so they have to combine this with a 'do as I do, not do as I say' policy on common areas. So, for example, a good leader should be prepared to come in early if staff are being asked to come in early to complete a special task, but won't necessarily be able to undertake every complex task that his or her staff members can.

MANAGEABILITY QUESTIONS

Manageability is a subtle issue. No one wants to take on a person who is going to be a constant irritation, and takes up so much management time that the manager might as well have done the job him or herself. However, many staff who are labelled difficult to manage are those that respond to different types of power (see the reference to French and Raven in the comments on leadership question 6). They are only difficult to manage if the wrong approach is taken to manage them. As much as possible, these questions should pick out those that are just difficult without the redeeming features – but some questions try to assess the types of power that are most suitable for managing this individual, as you won't always have a choice of the right type of manager available.

1. *Where do you want to be in five years' time?*

    A lot of potential value in this one. Does the interviewee have realistic aspirations (and self-valuation)? Does he or she understand what the sort of job that might be mentioned for the future implies? Is the current post seen as a stepping-stone, or an end in itself? Is the increasing move to flatter organizations with more opportunities for variety, but less for promotion, a good fit with his or her profile? If you get a blanket answer like 'in management', explore the candidate's understanding of what management is and why he or she wants to be involved in it – a particularly testing consideration.

2. *How do you feel about working 9 am–5 pm?*

    This is a useful question when dealing with a first-time job applicant. The interviewee may have little experience of regular working hours. Look for the ability to recognize this, but also what it takes to be regular (with any appropriate experience such as holiday jobs). If your company operates flexible hours and the interviewee mentions this (perhaps in the context of working better at certain times of day), it shows that your applicant has done his or her homework.

3. *How do you feel about being told you are doing something wrong?*

    Look for human understanding, rather than just parroting that he or she is always willing to take advice. A better reply would be something along the lines of, 'I think, like everyone, that I find it difficult sometimes when I'm criticized, but I have found that I can take helpful comments and feel good about doing things better. Occasionally I won't agree and then I'll say so and discuss the matter rather than hiding it away'. Worry about anyone who says, 'I can't ever remember being wrong' (and it does happen).

4. *Where are you prepared to work?*

If you are a multi-site company, or the job might involve travel, it is worth exploring the individual's attitudes. While it is less common now, not long ago many staff members below management level expected to have a job where they lived rather than moving to a job. In asking the question you are checking for flexibility and enthusiasm.

5. *How long do you want to stay with this company?*

Be suspicious of both those who expect a job for life, and those who see it as a year or two's stepping stone. The former will lack drive, while the latter will be concentrating more on job applications than on the task. The best answer is likely to be conditional on the company offering enough challenges, but with the expectation that it will be a long-term relationship (because it's a great company). Expect the more astute interviewees to turn this one round and ask what you think, or how long you've been with the company.

6. *How many hours a week do you think you should work?*

This verges on a shock question, as it puts the interviewee under considerable pressure. Most companies like to present an image of being caring and considerate to employees' needs, but is yours a company that expects everyone to work overly long hours? Be suspicious of anyone who is categorical about working the contracted hours. Probably the ideal answer is someone who will put in extra hours when there is a special requirement, but does expect a reasonable time away from work – you want balanced employees with fully rounded lives.

7. *How do you react to pressure at work?*

Look for a good example (if necessary prompt for it) of how the individual has managed to work under pressure. The answer should ideally include good time management, the ability to delegate and work with a team to distribute the load, and an enjoyment of occasional pressure, without being the sort of person who can't work without it.

8. *Could you do your current boss's job?*

A good test of the balance between confidence and hubris. Be suspicious of both those who could never do the job, and those who could do it better today. A good balance is for the individual to feel that they could, with the appropriate experience and training, aspire to the job should the occasion arise. However, don't be entirely dismissive of either extreme. It's a poor assumption that everyone should have the aspiration of achieving management. Some of the best workers love their job and want to remain productive rather than become administrative (doctors, for example).

9. *What would your ideal boss be like?*

   Explore the types of power and the management or leadership preferences of the individual. Does he or she prefer detailed direction or broad guidance? Would authority be the best way to direct them or charisma? Reward or being on the same technical wavelength? After his or her first response, try to get an understanding of why he or she feels these are the characteristics of a good boss.

10. *If you think a co-worker could do his or her job better, what would you do about it?*

    There's a fine line between being helpful and being a pain. We've all come across people who are constantly moaning about the way things are – and the way they should be. Look out for someone who is likely to be too free with his or her opinions, or constantly carping and complaining. A much better answer would be that the interviewee would discuss the situation with the other person, encouraging them to explore the problem, but never actually point out a fault or criticize (or complain to the boss).

SELF-STARTER QUESTIONS

Increasingly we are looking for self-starters, people who will just get on with the job, taking appropriate decisions without always coming back to ask for instructions. Such initiative might once have been seen as being 'difficult' – the army notoriously didn't like junior soldiers to think for themselves. However, the army is no longer a good model for business – more independent initiative is essential to cope with the pressures and constantly changing business environment.

1. *How and why did you get your previous jobs?*

   Whether you are talking work experience for first-timers, or 'real' jobs for the more experienced, there is considerable insight to be gained from looking into the process by which they got their jobs. Be a little wary. No one with any sense is going to say, 'My dad found it for me'. Equally, there is nothing wrong with someone working in the family firm for experience, as long as they can justify it fluently. Look out for someone taking the initiative, having a long-term view and being prepared to be flexible.

2. *What's the best example of your showing initiative?*

   Every candidate should have some good examples, though frighteningly a fair number are fazed by this question. Look for understanding of what initiative is required for, and the difference between showing initiative and being a pest by constantly challenging authority. Questions like this will often result in a longish pause while the interviewee collects his or her thoughts. This isn't a bad thing – it shows that the question is being taken seriously.

3. *How do you deal with time management?*

   The ideal here is a balanced answer. Someone who just gets by somehow or other is worryingly disorganized. On the other hand, someone who details every five minutes on a chart and ticks it off is liable to spend more time on time management than on the task – and is dangerously inflexible. You should be looking for someone who has a short, clear list of priorities for the day and/or week, which are challenging but usually met.

4. *How do you feel about your career so far?*

   You are probably looking for someone who will stick with the job, but you don't want a candidate without ambition, so the ideal reply should suggest that the individual has made good progress, and is happy to take things at the right pace, but expects more still. If yours is a relatively flat organization, look for appreciation of variety and personal growth rather than simply looking for promotions.

5. *Do you prefer to be absolutely clear about what is expected of you, or to work within broad principles?*

   Be careful to phrase this one so that the two options are equally weighted. You aren't going to get a lot of information by asking, 'Do you prefer to be lead by the nose, or to act with initiative?' There isn't a right answer here, it really does depend on the job, although an increasing number of positions do depend on individuals being able to act flexibly and with initiative.

6. *What would you do if you came to work one day with nothing scheduled, and weren't given any guidance of what to do?*

   Time management has to be goal-oriented. Some individuals are excellent at managing to fill their time without ever producing anything. This question probes the candidate's ability to go and find something to do if nothing is scheduled.

7. *What makes for an effective meeting?*

   All too often a lot of time is wasted in meetings with no clear agenda, where conversations are allowed to stray all over the place and no actions are generated. Look out for an understanding of these prime points (clear agenda, meeting well chaired to follow the agenda, action points produced and followed up) from the candidate.

8. *How do you choose what you are going to wear for a particular business occasion?*

   There was a time when there was nothing to choose, but these days there is much more flexibility. The self-starter should be trying to do two things: to put across a personal image, and to fit the expectations of the others involved (whether in an interview, or a meeting with a customer or whatever). If there is anything notable about the way they have dressed for the interview, explore this.

9. *Your boss asks you to assess a new potential supplier. The company doesn't come up to expectations. What would you do?*

   A low initiative response would be to go back to the boss with this information and wait for instructions. The self-starter would consider checking out alternatives and go back to the boss with a range of options, rather than simple failure.

10. *Your boss is due to attend an important meeting, but does not arrive at work that morning. What do you do?*

Again this question is looking for the self-starter's ability to assess needs and take action. He or she should probably try to contact the boss (mobile phone, home), but if it's impossible, to get whatever information they can together and either attend the meeting on the boss's behalf or discuss the possibility with the other attendees (being sure not to drop the boss in it). Look for both initiative and social understanding here.

CREATIVITY QUESTIONS

Creativity is an essential ability in practically any role in modern business. The speed of change, the need for flexibility, the ever-increasing competition, all make creativity something that can't be overlooked when interviewing.

1. *What types of books do you read, and why?*

   It doesn't really matter what types of books are read as long as there's a good breadth, and a mix of fiction and non-fiction. Don't be negative just because a particular genre doesn't fit your own reading preferences. Instead, look for a good explanation of the appeal of the different types of books.

2. *If you had to come up with a new product or service for our company, what would it be?*

   A good opportunity for thinking out of the box, which also probes the candidate's understanding of what your company is all about. Look for something original that would mean a significant step forward for the company.

3. *How do we tend to stifle creativity in business?*

   An understanding of the ways that creativity tends to be stifled is a useful guide to the interviewee's understanding of the realities of being innovative in a business environment. Look for aspects like 'it has been tried before', not wanting to take risks, thinking there is only one right answer, and so on.

4. *Why is it important for a company like ours to be innovative?*

   Although the specifics of the answer will vary, any company these days has reasons for needing creativity. Much will focus around differentiation (making the company better than the competition) and cost saving, but in the end it comes down to survival.

5. *Do you like taking risks?*

   This is a closed question, but it should be very easy to move on from a yes or no answer. The ideal reply is probably to say that the candidate doesn't like taking just any risk (showing they're not irresponsible) but recognizes that some calculated risk-taking is necessary if the company is to progress.

6. *How do you think the failure of a new idea should be treated?*

Another one digging into the understanding of the nature and value of calculated risk-taking. It is almost impossible to be creative without taking risks – and this implies failing sometimes. The reaction to failure should be to learn from the outcome, and move straight on. Failure, used correctly, is a positive tool for advancement. This one could be turned round on you, by the candidate asking if yours is the sort of company where it is safe to fail in the name of progress. Be prepared to answer.

7. *How could getting rid of a suggestion scheme improve the flow of ideas in a company?*

This one is designed to see how the candidate can actually think through a proposition and the nature of ideas. Suggestion schemes say, 'This is where you have ideas, now get back to your real job'. Getting rid of a suggestion scheme (along with the right message and mechanisms) can say, 'Having ideas is part of everybody's job, every day, rather than something you do in your spare time'.

8. *I'd like you to think a little creatively. Who would you say were the main competitors of luxury car manufacturer Mercedes Benz at the top of their product range?*

The clue is in the question. It's fine to come up with other luxury car manufacturers, but we have asked for a creative reply. Look for other competing high-end transport manufacturers (yachts, helicopters, private planes), and other luxury expenditures (holiday homes, swimming pools, etc).

9. *What would you say is the most creative thing you do?*

Look for a creative answer. It might be a traditional creative task (painting or writing or whatever), but it might just as easily be selling a company's products. If there's no explanation included, ask why the particular activity was chosen. If a hobby is chosen, ask for an example in the work context.

10. *How might a child's ideas be more valuable to the business than an expert's?*

There's a strange effect when an expert is called in. The expert knows exactly what is and isn't possible, so the expert won't consider lots of options that might be very valuable. The child hasn't these limitations, so will expect the impossible and suggest totally new directions. (For instance, Edwin Land's daughter asked him why she couldn't see the photograph he had taken right away – after the typical expert's answers occurred to him, he realized she was right and went on to develop the Polaroid camera.) The candidate won't have this technical feel for the proposition, but the creative candidate should be able to understand and explain the concept.

SHOCK QUESTIONS

The shock tactic can seem to be putting the applicant under too much stress – and care needs to be taken to ensure that it isn't just shock for the sake of it – but it can give a valuable assessment of how a candidate will react under pressure, and how much they are liable to take things at face value.

1. *What makes you the right person for this job?*

    This really shouldn't be a shock question, but a surprising number of applicants are not prepared for it and get flustered. The difficulty for the interviewees is partly that they are being asked to compare themselves against an unknown (the rest of the applicants) and also because they are being asked to sing their own praises, which few like to do.

2. *How will you add value to the company?*

    This is an alternative to, 'What do you think you will bring to the job?' that has a much harder edge. It is asking the candidate to justify his or her existence. Most interviewees will respond with generalisms. If you want to be even tougher, follow it up by saying something like, 'You are going to cost us X a year – how much financial benefit can we expect to get from you to offset this, and how will you contribute to that benefit?'

3. *What other jobs have you applied for? What would you do if they all offered you a position?*

    It may be that this is the candidate's only application: if so, ask why. Is it really the only suitable job on the market? Is he or she wildly over-confident or just testing the water? It's the follow up if there are other jobs that makes this a below-the-belt question, as it asks the interviewee to rank your job against the competition. Look for good reasoning, and an answer that gives some good points to your competitors (otherwise it would be fair to ask why he or she is applying to these competitors at all).

4. *Sell me one of our company's products or services.*

    It's only fair to give the interviewee a little thinking time here with this double nasty. You are expecting them to know something about one of your products and to sell it to you. It's reasonable for the interviewee to say, 'While I've got a good broad picture, can you tell me a little about a specific product you'd like me to sell?' This one tests communication skills and thinking on his or her feet. It's nasty but effective.

5. *Should you be earning more than you are?*

    An intentionally closed question; use silence first, then a probe if you get a single word answer. Whatever, make sure you get into the 'why' as well as the basic opinion. Look for an understanding that reward is not just about cash.

6. *Why should I recruit an outsider/someone from inside for this job?*

    A shock mostly because few interviewees will think of it. Whichever side of the coin they're on, they should be able to justify their value, either as bringing in fresh experience or building on internal knowledge.

7. *I'm not really sure this is the job for you.*

    A particularly nasty one this, expecting the candidate to be prepared to argue that, in fact, things are very different from this apparent perception. Be prepared to answer a response like, 'What makes you think that?' from the more astute interviewees.

8. *We're in a cost-cutting phase. Why shouldn't we scrap this job entirely?*

    The poor applicant has hardly got a toe into the company and you are making him or her redundant. This is a real think-on-your-feet question. Most candidates will have assumed the job has value to the company, or why would you be recruiting for it? Don't count it as negative if there's quite a pause for gathering thoughts; it's better to give a considered answer than steaming in without thinking.

9. *Is that all?*

    Or any similar question in a slightly derogatory tone after an answer, the implication being that the answer was incomplete or skimpy. This isn't the best way to get more out of the interviewee (something like, 'Could you expand on that?' or, 'Is there anything else you can tell me?' would be much better), but will usefully increase the pressure if you feel that the interviewee is not giving their all or needs to be tested under stress. Having a general purpose retort of, 'I just wanted to make sure you'd covered all the ground' or something similar will be valuable to have ready in case you get the response, 'Yes, what do you think I missed?'

10. *The current occupant of the job you are applying for is being dismissed for incompetence. If your first task for the company was to tell him this, what would you say?*

    Ouch. A very unlikely scenario (at least, that the current occupant should still be in the job unawares), but one that really puts the candidate on his or her toes and tests interpersonal skills.

ANALYTICAL THINKING QUESTIONS

Questions that expect the applicant to really think through a problem are increasing in popularity in interviews. They almost always involve a degree of stress. For a number of years, I interviewed for the Operational Research department at British Airways. As mentioned in the first chapter, the same analytical thinking question was used for a long period of time (it had been used in my own interview), and proved remarkably effective at sifting out original thinkers. That particular question is too technical to list here, but one useful trick it employed was that the answer required understanding rather than detailed working out. As something of a smokescreen, we always pointed out that one of the interviewers could provide assistance with (totally unnecessary) formulae if the candidate needed it. This backfired on me in my first experience as a junior interviewer when I was asked for the formula for standard deviation and my mind went totally blank. Always remember that the point of these questions is not to come to a particular answer, but to demonstrate appropriate reasoning.

1. *Why are US manhole covers round?*

    This is a classic analytical thinking question, the answer being that, unlike square or rectangular covers, round ones can't fall down the hole. US companies sometimes ask the variant, 'Why are manhole covers round', which suffers from implied cultural imperialism – in many countries this simply isn't true, and 'they aren't' is a perfectly valid answer if you ask that form of the question.

2. *A man fell out of a plane without a parachute or any other device. The ground below was rock hard, yet he plummeted 10,000 feet unharmed. How could this be?*

    One possibility is that the plane was more than 10,000 feet up. It's only in the last couple of feet that he gets harmed. The candidate may be able to think of an alternative reason – it doesn't matter what the answer is as long as the reasoning is good.

3. *Every lunchtime I turn up at a tube station any time between 12 noon and 1 pm. I catch the first train in either direction, as there are pubs I like to lunch at in both directions. Although the time I turn up is purely random, and trains in both directions operate with the same frequency, 9 times out of 10 I go to the westbound pub. Explain.*

    This sort of logical thinking problem comes much more naturally to some than to others, so encourage the candidate to think aloud and concentrate on the process rather than reaching the solution. Look for logical, analytical steps. The answer, should you need to explain it, is that trains run every 10 minutes in both directions. Eastbound trains come one minute after westbound, so for 9 out of every 10 minutes, the next train will be westbound.

4. *If you fill two buckets with water and take one to 20 degrees Celsius and the other to 20 degrees Fahrenheit, then simultaneously drop a coin into each, which will reach the bottom first?*

    The 20 degrees Celsius bucket. The other will never reach the bottom: the water is frozen. This question tests the candidate's ability to really listen to the requirement, otherwise they may rush off into all manner of complex consideration that is irrelevant.

5. *You put a single amoeba into a box and seal it up. Each minute the number of amoebae doubles. If the box is full an hour after starting the experiment, how long did it take to get half-full?*

    Again we're looking out for attention to what has been said. The number doubles in a minute, so the box goes from half-full to full in a minute, so it was half-full after 59 minutes (or one minute before it was full). Everyone should get there, but it's a matter of how quickly and logically.

6. *A man goes into a bar, sits down and orders a double brandy, three pints of beer and 10 glasses of water. 'Ah,' says the barmaid, 'you must be a fireman.' How does she know?*

    Because he was wearing his uniform. This sort of distraction puzzle is useful at seeing how well the candidate under pressure can see around the sort of irrelevancies that are often flung up when trying to understand a real life problem.

7. *A farmer has two large fields. One is two square kilometres, the other two kilometres square. Which, if either, is bigger?*

    Some people will simply know this, but others will exhibit good logical deduction in working out that two kilometres square (ie two kilometres each side of a square) is four square kilometres, and hence bigger. It's a very simple question, but not every job requires the same level of analytical skills.

8. *How could you tell which of two totally differently shaped sealed containers of soup (each with the same thickness of plastic in the container) held more without opening them?*

    Like Archimedes in the bath, put each container into a larger filled container of water and see which displaced more water. Shouting Eureka is optional. This question is more useful if the candidate is not a science student, making some working out necessary.

9. *Bearing in mind how many years have passed, and when metal alloys were first brought into use, estimate what percentage of the old coins dug up in the UK have AD dates stamped on them and what percentage have BC dates stamped on them.*

Again a handy check that someone really thinks about the question before rushing in to answer. Those who speak first and think later may say, 'I haven't got a clue' or attempt some dubious calculation. The more thoughtful will point out that there are hardly likely to be any coins with BC dates stamped on them, as that dating system clearly can't be contemporary.

10. *By coincidence, grandfather, father and son had birthdays in the same month. It was John's 1st birthday, Ted's 20th birthday and Bill's 42nd. John obviously couldn't buy cards, yet Ted got a 'happy birthday, Dad' card while Bill didn't. Explain.*

Bill was John's father, so didn't get a card. Ted was Bill's father so did get a card. Ted's birthday was 29th February, so though it was his 20th birthday, he was 80 years old. Mostly a matter of untangling this one, demonstrating a capability for juggling different pieces of information. Don't let the candidates write anything down.

7

OTHER SOURCES

FINDING OUT MORE

Interviewing is a broad requirement that takes in a wide range of skills from the interpersonal to the organizational. *Instant Interviewing* will have given you an exposure to the critical core skills, but if you would like to go into further depth, the books recommended below will give you some guidance.

An easy way to get hold of many of the recommended books is through the Creativity Unleashed online bookshop, which specializes in business and creativity books. See **http://www.cul.co.uk/books**

GENERAL INTERVIEWING
These guides to interview techniques will help to round out your skills.

Margaret Dale, *How to be a Better Interviewer*, Kogan Page, 1996
A very structured guide to improving your interviewing skills, particularly around recruitment. Lots of detail and quite readable.

Robert Edenborough, *Effective Interviewing*, Kogan Page, 1999
A broad guide to the skills needed in interviewing, whatever the application. There is a fair amount of detail; the book provides excellent background reading on the interviewing, and a fair number of the skills, techniques and applications that it promises.

John Fletcher, *Conducting Effective Interviews*, Kogan Page, 1995
Lots of bullet points and lists, but not the checklist-driven approach that is usual in the 'Better Management Skills' series. Covers all interviewing styles at a very summary level, despite the snappy subtitle 'Reduce staff turnover and match the candidate to the job through more effective recruitment, retention and redeployment'.

Daphne Keats, *Interviewing,* Open University Press, 2000
This book is good on the basics of interviewing, giving a lot of detail on interviewing different types of subject. It covers interviews in general, not just business or recruitment, but has plenty of useful information.

Tony Pont and Gillian Pont, *Interviewing Skills for Managers*, Piatkus Books, 1998
The first part of this book deals with the general aspects of interviewing such as asking the right questions in the right manner, using the correct body language and listening well. The authors then focus on the main types of interview that a manager is likely to come across, including appraisal. A good all-rounder.

Laurence Smalley, *Interviewing and Selecting High Performers*, Kogan Page, 1997
This is from the 'Practical Guidebook' series by California-based organizational improvement consultants, Richard Chang Associates. It's a handy, step-by-step practical guide to the needs of anyone who is recruiting staff. Least convincing is the 'high performers' bit – high performers tend to be mould-breakers, while this is very much about recruiting to fit the mould.

BEING INTERVIEWED

The book recommended here isn't just helpful for interview candidates. It can give you inspiration on questions to ask – and also helps you to be aware just how a well-prepared interviewee could handle the questions that you think will take them by surprise.

Martin John Yate, *Great Answers to Tough Interview Questions*, Kogan Page, 1998
This book has been going since the 1980s and is now in its fourth edition, selling over 3 million copies. It concentrates on interviewing from the interviewee's viewpoint – the *Financial Times*, for instance, describes it as 'the best book on job-hunting generally'. It is a valuable resource for the interviewer, both by identifying question styles and directions to take – but also as a guide to some of the misleading, preprogrammed answers you are liable to get from a reader of a book like this so that you can counter them.

INFORMATION AND KNOWLEDGE

Interviewing is a process of extracting and processing information. Skills to help with this come from many sources and directions – this wide-ranging introductory collection will help with your information collation and knowledge management.

Tony and Barry Buzan, *The Mind Map Book*, BBC Books, 1993
A beautifully illustrated guide to the use of mind maps to take notes, structure ideas and aid memory. Written by Tony Buzan, the developer of the mind map concept, this is the ultimate guide for the note taker.

Brian Clegg, *Instant Brainpower*, Kogan Page, 1999
This book in the 'Instant' series is an ideal complement to *Instant Interviewing* as it builds on some key skills that are essential to interviewing – memory, knowledge handling and innate creative ability. A wide range of exercises make enhancing your thinking skills enjoyable and effective.

Brian Clegg, *Mining the Internet*, Kogan Page, 1999
Being able to use the World Wide Web to harvest information, and using e-mail as an effective means of communication and getting information from others is an essential skill for the 21st century interviewer. This very readable book guides you through making best use of these amazing information resources.

Brian Clegg, *The Chameleon Manager*, Butterworth Heinemann, 1998
This book examines the requirements that all managers will need in the 21st century world of flexible working, where there is no such thing as a job for life. With three key concepts of creativity, communication and knowledge, it provides a skill base that is ideal both for the interviewer and as a help for developing your own career.

Mariana Funes and Nancy Johnson, *Honing Your Knowledge Skills*, Butterworth Heinemann, 1998
Combines some detailed techniques for expanding your knowledge management skills with a lot of the theory underlying it. Particularly appropriate for the interviewer are the skills needed to extract information, but the whole area of knowledge handling is of importance.

SELLING

Your role as interviewer is not purely one of selector. A great candidate is liable to be offered a number of jobs – it is as much your role to sell the company and the job to him or her as it is to assess the candidate's value. These books will help with the sales and customer service skills to make this possible.

Jay Abraham, *Getting Everything You Can Out of All You've Got*, Piatkus Books, 2000
A paean of the wonders of selling from the man aptly referred to as the greatest marketing expert alive. Abraham's style is sometimes irritatingly inspirational, but his content is second to none. This book is almost guaranteed to change the way you go about selling yourself, a job or the benefits of working for your company.

Brian Clegg, *Capturing Customers' Hearts*, FT Prentice Hall, 2000
This book examines what it is about a company, its products, its brands and its people that wins over customers. It examines 12 components of charisma – the property that enables a company or product to sell itself to the customer. Capturing an interviewee's heart is increasingly necessary as companies compete for the top employees; in this respect, good candidates are as much customers as anyone buying in a shop.

Richard Denny, *Selling to Win*, revised 2nd edn, Kogan Page, 2000
A very practical, very readable book that takes away the mystery from selling. Full of useful insights, there's a tried and tested technique here for every occasion.

MOTIVATION

Aligned with selling, motivation is at the heart of the sales pitch you make in attempting to make a top-rank candidate join your organization rather than another.

John Allan, *How to be Better at Motivating People*, Kogan Page, 1996
An Industrial Society-backed guide to motivation. Good use of case studies and tips make this a good choice to accompany *Instant Motivation* (see below).

Brian Clegg, *Instant Motivation*, Kogan Page, 2000
A companion volume in the 'Instant' series, *Instant Motivation* provides over 70 techniques and skills to get individuals, teams and large groups better in line with your aspirations. An excellent adjunct to this book.

Richard Denny, *Motivate to Win*, Kogan Page, 1993
Don't be put off by the relative age of this book; the content hasn't dated. Denny has a very charismatic approach to motivation, and puts the message across well. It's a personal approach, so some may not like it, but it's worth a look.

David Firth, *How to Make Work Fun*, Gower, 1995
David Firth's book explores the whole area of fun and work, a key to effective motivation. The A to Z format seems a little forced occasionally, but makes it easy to dip into. While not always directly practical, it's a great source of inspiration.

Patrick Forsyth, *30 Minutes to Motivate Your Staff*, Kogan Page, 1998
Part of a pocket book series putting across the basics of the subject – handy if you'd like a bit more than the introductory chapters that *Instant Motivation* can give, but haven't time for a Denny or an Allan.

Robert Heller, *Motivating People*, Dorling Kindersley, 1998
A handy pocket guide to motivation in the heavily illustrated DK style. Some of the approaches are a trifle old-fashioned, but overall a good pocket introduction to the subject.

Michael Leapman, *The Last Days of the Beeb*, Coronet, 1987
Leapman's inside view of the BBC before the major reorganizations that turned it into a modern business is a classic case study in how not to motivate. Well worth reading.

Ricardo Semler, *Maverick!*, Arrow, 1994
One of the best books ever written about motivation. It's not a textbook, but the biography of a company. Despite being located in Brazil during runaway inflation and with potentially difficult unions, Semler took a disgruntled workforce and totally changed their motivation by making the workplace somewhere they wanted to be.

STRESS MANAGEMENT

Two exercises from *Instant Stress Management* are included in this book for a very good reason. Interviewing is a stressful process, for the interviewer as much as the interviewee. Being able to do something about that stress is helpful both for the interviewer, who may need protection from damaging stress (and hence discover that he or she actually enjoys interviewing), and for the interviewee, who will get entirely the wrong message if the interviewer appears nervous or stressed. The books listed here provide a good guide to making the best of stress.

David Ashton, *The 12-Week Executive Health Plan*, Kogan Page, 1993
Good health is one of the cornerstones of being able to manage stress. This readable book, which manages to avoid the tendency of the health movement to work with the fad-of-the-moment, is a good guide to getting something practical done about improving your health.

Brian Clegg, *Instant Stress Management*, Kogan Page, 2000
One of the most popular titles in the 'Instant' series, *Instant Stress Management* helps to bring the stress of interviewing under control. Recognizing that one of the main stressors is time pressure, it provides over 70 techniques that can be taken on board in a few minutes, handling stress when and where it occurs.

Cary L. Cooper, Rachel Cooper and Lynn Eaker, *Living with Stress*, Penguin, 1991
A good exploration of stress, what it is and where it comes from. Although not specifically business-oriented, it spends quite a lot of time on workplace stress, including some slightly dated but nonetheless useful research. Includes DIY stress questionnaires to assess your condition.

Lynn Fossum, *Managing Anxiety*, Kogan Page, 1993
A quick guide to the nature of anxiety and how to conquer it. Fossum's book is short and has plenty of practical exercises to reduce this key component of stress.

Brenda O'Hanlon, *Stress: The Commonsense Approach*, Newleaf, 1998
A good pocketbook giving a general overview of stress and dealing with it. Gives rather a lot of space to alternative treatments and therapy, but otherwise well-balanced.

TIME MANAGEMENT

Time management is the Cinderella of management skills. It seems dowdy and unattractive, but getting it right is at the heart of so much business success. It is doubly essential in interviewing – both in making the time for what is often an extra activity on top of your normal work, and for ensuring that time within the interview is managed well. Two techniques from *Instant Time Management* are included in this book. These books look at putting time management in its right place, making it less of a chore and more of an essential feature of life.

Brian Clegg, *Instant Time Management*, Kogan Page, 1999
A companion volume in the 'Instant' series, *Instant Time Management* provides a host of techniques for improving your time management without taking up too much time over it. Good time management enables you to deliver on your promises and ensures that your interviewing is successful.

Marion E. Hayes, *Make Every Minute Count*, 3rd edn, Kogan Page, 2000
In the quick-fire 'Better Management Skills' series, this in the only one of these books that is US-written, but the subject varies little between countries. Even more checklists and questionnaires than Smith's book, but this is an excellent way of getting started in the subject.

Ted Johns, *Perfect Time Management*, Arrow, 1994
A handy pocket book giving an overview of time management practice from a very pragmatic viewpoint. Varies between background and quite a lot of detail (eg suggested forms for the agenda of a meeting).

Lothar J Seiwert, *Managing Your Time*, Kogan Page, 1989
A very visual book with lots of diagrams, plans and cartoons – it'll either impress you (as it has apparently more than 300,000 readers) or leave you cold. Particularly helpful if you like very specific guidance and information as juicy snippets.

Jane Smith, *How to be a Better Time Manager*, Kogan Page, 1997
An Industrial Society-sponsored volume, Smith's book takes an easy-to-read, nononsense approach to time management. A fair number of checklists and little questionnaires to fill in along the way, if you like that style.

NON-VERBAL COMMUNICATION

Finding out more about body language is a vital aid to successful interviewing. Don't just go on what has been spoken; note what the body says, too.

Adrian Furnham, *Body Language at Work*, Institute of Personnel and Development, 1999
A more focused title than some, though it gives a less effective general introduction, looking at body language in the work context. Includes a section on detecting office liars and fakes, a particularly interesting angle for the interviewer.

Desmond Morris, *Manwatching*, Panther Books, 1978
Morris's classic coffee table book on human behaviour might seem a little pictorially dated by now, but his observations on human interaction are still spot on, and the wider brief, covering all interaction, not just body language, puts body language into an effective context.

Alan Pease, *Body Language*, Sheldon Press, 1997
A very readable and approachable introduction to non-verbal communication and its implications. Takes a wider view than may be necessary here, but an excellent starting point.

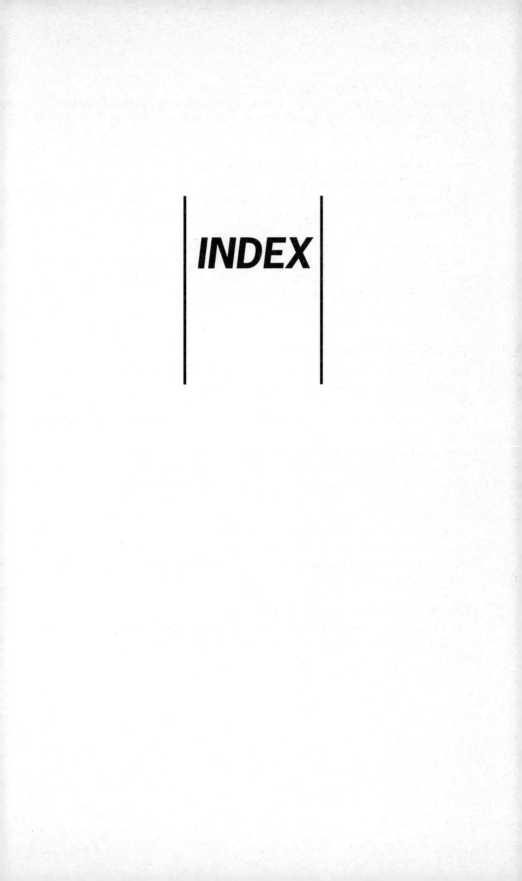

INDEX

12-Week Executive Health Plan, The 111
30 Minutes to Motivate Your Staff 110

aggression *see also* pressure, putting under
  as abuse of power 6
  as part of interview technique 6
  stretching interviewee 7
applicants, comparison of 4
applications, sifting *see also* recruitment
    precursors
  candidate's message 16–17
  exclusion criteria 16–17
  handwriting analysis 8, 17
  presentation of application 16
  visual exclusion 16

bibliography 107–12
Body Language 113
body language 26
  eye contact 26
  facial expressions 26
  looking relaxed 26
  non-verbal messages 26
Body Language at Work 113
breaks and chunks *see* stress-relief tactic(s)
breathing 37 *see also* stress
  calm-inducing 37
  exercises 37
  two types of 37
British Airways 7
Buzan, Tony 23

candidate, appearance of 21
  analysing own reactions 21
  bias 21
  dress sense 21
candidates, comparisons between 31
  experience v qualifications 31
  option evaluation 31 *see also* option
    evaluation, simple
Capturing Customers' Hearts 109
chairs, grouping of 9, 63
Chameleon Manager, The 108
checklist, environment 5, 60–66
  appropriate office/location 61
  chairs/tables, arranging 63–64
  clock, position of 64–65
  dress code 65
  e-mail queries, consideration of 61–62
  hospitality 65–66
  keep-out signs 63

notepads/pens 64
  personal preparation 65
  telephone interviews 62
  telephones, disconnecting 62–63
checklist, information 5, 49–55
  application form 52
  external recruitment 54 *see also*
    recruitment, external
  goals 51
  internal interview 55 *see also*
    interview, internal
  interview plan 51–52
  interviewee's CV 52
  job description 53 *see also main entry*
  key questions 51 *see also* key
    questions, planning
  letter of invitation 53
  test results 52–53 *see also main entry*
checklist, selling 6, 69–76
  advancement, opportunities for 74
  car parking/public transport 73
  career flexibility 74–75
  company brochures 71
  details of package 71
  dress code 72
  equipment 74
  flexible working options 71–72
  food facilities 73
  office space 72–73
  perks 75–76
  relocating, support for 76
  social facilities 74
  support options for workforce 72
  training 75
  travel 75
  workplace tours 76
communication, non-verbal 27
  body language 27
  eye contact 27
comparisons, fair 44
  buffer times 44
  interview panel 44
  prejudice 44
  sequence of interviews 44
Conducting Effective Interviews 107
Creativity Unleashed Web site
  (www.cul.co.uk/software) 30
criteria *see* applications, sifting; job,
  understanding the *and* option
    evaluation
CV, the perfect 18

CV *continued*
  as communication vehicle   18
  modelling on own CV   18
  tips for   18

data   *see* information

Effective Interviewing   107
Entranet   35
environment checklist   *see* checklist,
  environment

feedback to candidate   45
  advice for future   45
  criteria for decision   45
  interview notes   45
Financial Times   108
foundation skills   4, 11–45
  applications, sifting   *see main entry*
  assessing test results   *see* test results,
    assessing
  breaks   *see* stress-relief tactics
  breathing is good for you   *see* breathing
    and stress
  comparing apples and oranges   *see*
    candidates, comparisons between
    and option evaluation
  CV, the perfect   *see main entry*
  fair comparisons   *see* comparisons, fair
  graphical notes   *see main entry*
  job, understanding the   *see main entry*
  journalists' tricks   *see main entry*
  key questions, planning   *see main entry*
  meeting and greeting   *see* meeting/
    greeting (welcome)
  non-verbal replies   *see* body language
  note taking   *see main entry*
  offer letter   *see main entry*
  open questions   *see main entry*
  option evaluation, simple   *see main entry*
  option evaluation, sophisticated   *see main
    entry*
  Pareto   *see* Pareto analysis
  recovering rejection   *see* rejection
  scheduling interviews   *see* interviews
  taking up references   *see* references
  top 10 list   *see* time management
  turning up the pressure   *see* pressure,
    putting under
  using silence   *see* silence, using

what do they look like?   *see* candidate,
  appearance of
your body   *see* body language

*Getting Everything You Can Out of All
  You've Got*   109
graphical notes   7, 23
  as interviewing aid   23
  exercise in   23
  keeping focus   23
  mind mapping   23
Great Answers to Tough Interview Questions
  108

Honing your Knowledge Skills   109
How to be a Better Interviewer   107
How to be a Better Time Manager   113
How to be Better at Motivating People
  109
How to Make Work Fun   110

information
  as currency of interview   5
  checklist   *see* checklist, information
  information v data   5
  sources of (bibliography)   107–12
Instant Brainpower   23, 108
Instant Interviewing   3
Instant Motivation   109
Instant Negotiation   30
Instant Stress Management   35, 37, 110
Instant Time Management   35, 111
interview, internal   55   *see also* checklist,
  information
  discussion with colleagues   55
  performance appraisals   55
interview environment   5
  importance of   5
interviewers   9
  human resources/personnel   9
  number of   9
  technical guidance   9
Interviewing   107
interviewing   1–9
  giving interviewee time to prepare   8
  positive benefits of   6
  psychometric test(s)   4
  telephone   8
Interviewing and Selecting High Performers
  107

interviewing skills
  for manager(s)   3
  in recruitment   3
  traditional line management   3
Interviewing Skills for Managers   107
interviews   3, 4–5, 43
  lunch, importance of   43
  number of   43
  organic   5
  preparation   3
  scheduling   43
  structured   4–5

job, understanding the   14–15
  criteria, setting   15
  evaluation exercises   15
  job description *see main entry*
  sophisticated option evaluation exercise
      15
job description   14, 53
  practice in absorbing   14
  writing   14
journalists' tricks   25
  evasion   25
  exploring points   25
  prepared questions   25

key questions, planning   19, 51
  creating sense of flow   19
  mind map   19

Last Days of the Beeb, The   110
Living with Stress   111

Make Every Minute Count   111
Managing Anxiety   111
Managing Your Time   113
Manwatching   113
Maverick!   110
meeting/greeting (welcome)   20
  as pleasant experience   20
  outline of interview structure   20
Mind Map Book, The   23, 108
mind map(ping)   19, 23, 79
Mining the Internet   108
Motivate to Win   110
Motivating People   110

note taking   7, 22, 23
  graphical notes   7, 22, 23

importance of   22
practice   22
steering notes   7
tapes   7

offer letter   41
  elements of   41
  following up verbal offer   41
open questions   24
  rephrasing closed questions   24
  yes or no questions   24
option evaluation, simple   29, 31
  logical criteria   29
  scoring against criteria   29
  software   30 *see also* Creativity
      Unleashed Web site
option evaluation, sophisticated   15, 29, 30
  intuition   30
  systematic approach   30
  weighting criteria   30
organic interview *see* interviews, organic

Pareto, Vilfredo   36
Pareto Analysis   36, 49
  80:20 rule   36
  application and use of   36
Paxman, Jeremy   80
Perfect Time Management   112
performance appraisals
  internal   6, 55
personality profiles   9
  Myers Brigg Type Indicator   9
pressure, putting under   6, 7, 33–34
  aggression   6
  debriefing   33
  group exercises   33
  role-play   7, 9, 33
  surroundings   33
psychometric test(s) *see* interviewing

question file   77–104 *see also* questions
  managing flow   80
  mind map   79
  prepared form of   79
  selecting questions   79
questions
  analytical thinking   102–04
  business awareness   85–86
  creativity   98–99
  general personality   81–82

questions *continued*
  key *see* key questions
  leadership 89–91
  manageability 92–94
  open *see* open questions
  self-starter 95–97
  shock 100–01
  skills 83–84
  teamwork 87–88
  verbal skills, testing 24

recruitment 4, 8–9 *see also* applications,
    sifting
  alongside interview 9
  precursors 8
  handwriting analysis 8
  personality profiles *see main entry*
  role-play 9
  sifting mechanisms *see main entry*
  telephone interviewing 8
recruitment, external 54 *see also*
    checklist, information
  details of former company 54
  information on own company 54
references 39–40
  aim of taking up 39
  letter v fax/e-mail/telephone 39
  offer subject to 39
  security checks on 39
  working characteristics 39
rejection 42
  candidate's needs/wishes 42
  change of heart, possibilities for 42
  proof of intent 42
role-play 7, 9 *see also* pressure, putting
    under

selling/selling checklist *see* checklist,
    selling

Selling to Win 109
sifting mechanisms 8 *see also* recruitment
    precursors
  academic results 8
  experience 8
  handwriting analysis 8
  telephone interviewing 8
silence, using 32
  constructively 32
  effectiveness/one-to-one 32
  practice 32
skills
  communication 13
  foundation *see* foundation skills
  interviewing *see* interviewing skills
sources of information *see* information,
    sources of
stress 6, 13, 37, 38 *see also* breathing and
    stress-relief tactic(s)
  stress management techniques 6, 13, 37
Stress: The Commonsense Approach 111
stress-relief tactic(s) 37, 38 *see also*
    breathing
  breaks and chunks 38
  change of activity 38
structured interview *see* interview,
    structured

test results 28, 52–53
  as filter 28
  how to make best use of 28
test results, assessing 28
  numerical skills 28
  personality profile 28
  technical aptitude 28
  verbal reasoning 28
time management 13, 35
  changing the list 35
  list of top 10 concerns 35

Visit Kogan Page on-line

Comprehensive information on
Kogan Page titles

Features include

- complete catalogue listings,
  including book reviews and
  descriptions

- on-line discounts on a variety
  of titles

- special monthly promotions

- information and discounts on
  NEW titles and BESTSELLING titles

- a secure shopping basket facility
  for on-line ordering

- infoZones, with links and
  information on specific areas of
  interest

PLUS everything you need to know
about KOGAN PAGE

http://www.kogan-page.co.uk